D0742903

THE OPEN-HEARTED WAY
TO OPEN ADOPTION

THE OPEN-HEARTED WAY
TO OPEN ADOPTION

Helping Your Child Grow Up Whole

**Lori Holden
with Crystal Hass**

ROWMAN & LITTLEFIELD PUBLISHERS, INC.
Lanham • Boulder • New York • Toronto • Plymouth, UK

Published by Rowman & Littlefield Publishers, Inc.
A wholly owned subsidiary of The Rowman & Littlefield Publishing Group, Inc.
4501 Forbes Boulevard, Suite 200, Lanham, Maryland 20706
www.rowman.com

10 Thornbury Road, Plymouth PL6 7PP, United Kingdom

British Library Cataloguing in Publication Information Available

Library of Congress Cataloging-in-Publication Data Available

ISBN 978-1-4422-1738-6 (cloth : alk. paper)—ISBN 978-1-4422-1740-9 (electronic)

♾ The paper used in this publication meets the minimum requirements of American National Standard for Information Sciences Permanence of Paper for Printed Library Materials, ANSI/NISO Z39.48-1992.

Printed in the United States of America

To Roger, who is learning right alongside me and who often tutors me on concepts that require the most patience. We're a team, you and I.

To Tessa and Reed, our steadfast professors, who offer us equal measures of wisdom and play. To the moon and back.

To my parents, Fred and Dottie, and my sisters, Sheri and Tami, who form the best cheering section a person could ever want.

To Crystal and Joe, Michele and AJ, who are, literally, miracle makers.

And to Melissa, who saw in me my telos. And to whom I grant exclusive twibbon rights.

—Lori

To Tessa and Tyler. You've made me the person I am. You are my angels on earth.

—Crystal

I've learned that whenever I decide something with an open heart I usually make the right decision.

—Maya Angelou

CONTENTS

Foreword   ix
   Carolyn Savage

Acknowledgments   xiii

Introduction   1

PART I: FROM FEAR TO FAMILY: PARENTS COME TOGETHER   9

1 What Is Open Adoption?   11

2 What to Consider When Choosing an Agency or Adoption
   Professional   27

3 The Parents in an Open Adoption   47

4 Guideposts from Families Who Have Traveled the Path   67

PART II: ORIENTING ON THE CHILD: OPEN ADOPTION'S TRUE NORTH 87

5 Openness and the Adoptee   89

6 Heading toward Wholeness: Integrating Your Child's
   Biology and Biography   109

7 Reality Check: When It's Not Easy   131

8 Openness in Foster, International, and Donor Situations   153

9 Especially for Birth Parents (and Those Who Want to
   Connect with Them)   167

10 Fare Well   179

Appendix A: Insight on Adoption Profiles   183

Appendix B: Opening Your Heart   189

Resources   191

Notes   197

Bibliography   205

Index   209

About the Author   211

FOREWORD

Carolyn Savage

On September 24, 2009, I gave the greatest gift of my life. It was on that day that I placed my fourth-born child in the arms of his forever mother. In that moment, I closed my eyes, took a deep breath, and jumped onto a road I thought I'd never travel: Would she keep me informed about his life? Would she love him as much as I do? Would he be happy? Questions flooded my mind while fears of tragic outcomes and eventual regrets plagued many of my thoughts. I knew I was doing the right thing for this child. My decision was rooted in love, but placing my baby in the care of another family for the rest of his life required a giant leap of faith. To say that I was scared would be an epic understatement.

If you are a birth parent or expectant parent considering open adoption for your child, I've stood in your shoes. *The Open-Hearted Way to Open Adoption* has been written for you.

Then, on August 11, 2011, I *received* the greatest gift of my life. When our twin daughters were placed in my arms by their first mother, I embarked on another road I'd thought I'd never travel, and the questions came again: Am I capable of being the best mother to these two precious girls? Could I bring my A-game to their lives and live up to the expectations of their first mother? How will I honor their first mother throughout their lives? I wanted them to know her and to understand their story. The day I left the hospital with my twin daughters, I was excited and intimidated. I needed to get this right for my girls and their first mother. Another leap of faith, and, again, I was scared.

If you are an adoptive or *prospective* adoptive parent considering open adoption as a way to build your family, I've stood in your shoes. And *The Open-Hearted Way to Open Adoption* has been written for you, too.

How does one woman find herself in both the shoes of a birth mother and a forever mother in one lifetime? My journey to parenthood has followed a very unique path. It began with the "old-fashioned" conceptions and births of our first two children. Then, after an eleven-year struggle with secondary infertility, we welcomed our third child into the world after a successful in-vitro fertilization. It wasn't until we headed back to our fertility specialist, in an attempt to use our remaining cryopreserved embryos, that my story took an unexpected turn. My fertility clinic made a mistake, thawing and transferring another couple's embryos, leaving me pregnant with a child that wasn't genetically mine. When I learned of the mix-up, only seconds after being told I was pregnant, I made an immediate decision: I'd carry this child and reunite him with his rightful parents. It was an easy decision based on the *do unto others* way I live my life, but that is where the easy part ended and my struggle began. My love for the baby I carried had nothing to do with DNA. I couldn't bear the thought of saying goodbye forever. I needed to know him. I wanted him to know me. As a result, I plunged into a journey much like an open adoption.

Before my pregnancy with the child of another couple, I'd never seriously delved into the nuances of open adoption. Of course, during my husband's and my ten years of trying to conceive I had looked into the option. Inevitably my research sessions would end with my dismissing it, intimidated by the formalities of the process. I found the notion of lawyers, contracts, and social workers overwhelming, and I was also frightened of getting my heart broken. The all-too-public failed adoptions that I'd seen unfold in the media had made quite an impression. Contributing to my trepidation was the concept of *open* adoption. Did *open* mean my child would have an additional mom and dad? The idea of navigating a relationship with another set of parents was something I didn't want to open my heart to . . . that is, until I became a mother who had to give up her baby. It was then that my circumstances caused a sudden change of heart.

Of course, I didn't technically place my child for adoption. I was thrust into an unprecedented set of circumstances that required me to surrender my baby, and I completely understood the logic of why that had to happen. Unfortunately that logic never fully translated to my heart. My maternal instincts didn't care about genetic technicalities. Like any birth mother, I loved my child the minute I learned he was coming to me, and I wanted the very best for his life. I desired to have an open relationship with his genetic family but was clueless what that would look like.

The concept of an open relationship with my baby's genetic parents scared me because of the countless possible pitfalls. I wanted to be part of his life but didn't want to intrude. I struggled with boundaries and fears of crossing them. If I pressed too hard, his family might shut me out. If I didn't press enough, his family might think I didn't care. In fact, I wasn't the only one fretting about the situation. Everyone involved was walking on eggshells, afraid of hurting the other or doing the wrong thing. A road map would have been a welcomed relief.

Two years after giving birth and saying goodbye to my fourth child, the tables of my reproductive life took a 180-degree turn. It was then that I found myself standing in a delivery room waiting for our gestational carrier to give birth to our twin daughters. Jennifer, our carrier, had been through so much with us. We cared deeply for her and were determined to honor her contribution to our daughters' lives. I wanted my children to know Jennifer and what she had done for them. I also was well aware that, even though Jennifer had chosen to be our gestational carrier, saying goodbye after delivery would be difficult for her. She loved my daughters and wanted the best for their lives. I felt like it was my duty not only to keep her informed but also to make sure she played a significant forever role. But what would that look like? A road map would have been a welcomed relief here, too.

I wish I had been able to read *The Open-Hearted Way to Open Adoption* earlier in my journey. Lori Holden's advice about navigating adoption with an open heart is priceless. It is sensitively written, honoring all parties of the adoption relationship. For birth mothers it provides reassuring advice regarding what to look for in an open-adoption agreement and how to proceed once your baby has been placed. Permission is granted for you to have expectations with regard to your baby and your futures together. More important, your sadness and sacrifice—as well as the gift of the chance to parenting that you are giving—are equally acknowledged.

And for adoptive parents, Lori's book lifts the veil on a healthy open-adoption relationship. Permission is granted for you to celebrate the birth of your baby or the welcoming of your child, and you'll receive powerful advice about the importance of communication before the match, while you're waiting for the birth, and throughout the life of your adoptive child.

In this book you'll find a realistic picture painted of open adoption. There are no promises of perfect journeys. Instead roadmaps are provided for likely detours and potential obstacles. For every bump along the way, Lori Holden and her daughter's birth mom, Crystal Hass, give firsthand insights into the emotions of every member involved in the adoption relationship.

Most important, Lori and Crystal remind everyone that the goal of an open adoption should always be focused on the best interests of the child and on seeing through the child's eyes. Lori's commitment to not sever her children's biology from their biography not only lays the groundwork for what an open-hearted approach requires but also reminds all the adults involved how critically important they are in the life of the adopted child.

I'm still embroiled in the earliest stages of my journey. I'm happy to report that we have a wonderful relationship with my fourth child's genetic family, and I think as he gets older he will know who I am. Jennifer continues to be an integral part of my daughters' young lives. By no means has my journey been effortless, but reading *The Open-Hearted Way to Open Adoption* has provided me with a powerful tool to make it less complicated and more navigable. That is why this book is a must-read for anyone contemplating building their family through adoption or third-party reproduction.

Carolyn Savage is author of Inconceivable: A Medical Mistake, the Baby We Couldn't Keep, and Our Choice to Deliver the Ultimate Gift *(2010). Additional information about her journey can be found at Inconcievablebook.com.*

ACKNOWLEDGMENTS

This part—simple thank-yous—should be the easiest section of a book to write. But envisioning all the people who have offered their love and influence and lessons during this book's journey makes me a more than a little *verklepmt*. I've been abundantly blessed by the people around me.

It all began with Fred and Dottie, my parents, who gave my sisters and me many gifts, one of the best being a deep belief in ourselves. From my dad I get my seeking, inquisitive nature, and from my mom I get my ability to abide. My sisters, Sheri and Tami, have been with me nearly all my life, always making me laugh, getting me fit, and bringing me their wise perspectives. Tami also serves as my superfantabulous book publicist. Sheri and Tami had the good sense (and good luck) to bring into our lives Tom, Jake, Ben, Ross, Gino, Dominic, and Eleana. I love you all.

Roger, already a writer when I met him, taught me from our early days about creativity (just do it!), spontaneity (an unplanned honeymoon backpacking through Europe), and talent (we all have it in all areas, in varying degrees). He supported me in writing this book by cooking countless dinners for our family, keeping the children occupied when I needed to focus, and by knowing, even when I didn't, that I would succeed in bringing this book to life. I am in awe of his abilities as a dad. I love you.

Tessa and Reed, my two muses. They, too, bring out the spontaneous in me, getting me out of my work comfort zone and leading me to play. I do not fully understand how I got to be so fortunate, but I am supremely grateful that every step of my journey to being a mom led me to being *your* mom. I love you both with my whole heart.

Crystal has been my partner in open adoption and in manifesting this book. Thank you for getting this whole thing launched by choosing me to be the mom to your beloved Tessa and for cocreating this relationship with us with ease and grace. Joe, Michele, and AJ, thank you for your manifold contributions to Tessa and Reed then, now, and always.

I watched my friend Melissa Ford publish two books, one nonfiction and the other fiction. She did it while raising twins, being an attentive wife, serving a community of infertility bloggers, and while working a "real" job. Not only all that, but she had this crazy idea that *I* could write a book. Dreamer! Much love to you, my friend.

Luna and Andy were the first two who stepped forward to allow me to tell their stories. They have also been steadfast supporters of me, my parenting, and my blog. Their contributions were followed by Alicia, Amy, Andi, Angie, Annie, Bobbie, Brandy, Caitlin, Claudia, Danielle, Dawn, Ellen, Eric, Heather, Jeni, Jenn, Jennifer, Jessica C., Jessica O., Judy, Juli, Julie, Kami, Kate, Lisa, LisaAnne, Mac, Maggie, Marcy, Mary, Meg, Melissa, Monika, Nancy, Rachel, Rebecca, Robyn, Sara, Stephannie, Tara, and Torrejon. Thank you for entrusting me with your stories.

To the entire ALI community (Adoption/neonatal Loss/Infertility) I offer my gratitude. You gave your voices. You gave me courage to raise my voice. You so totally rock. To Dawn Davenport and Dawn Friedman, I appreciate your modeling curiosity, integrity, and compassion. To Debbie Schwartz, thank you for your time and insight as you served as this book's sounding board. To various first parents, adoptive parents, and adoptees who wrote so poignantly about your experiences, thank you for helping me get as close to walking in your shoes as was possible from my limited vantage point.

To my Vino Support Group—Jeannie, Rose, Michelle, Tami, Julia, and Maggie—and my Tribe, thank you for cheering me on, for grounding me, for connecting me. For my friends Elektra, Angèle, Kathy, Cheryl, Julie, Alice, and Margaret, thank you for traveling the path with me. To yoginis Andrea, Jane, Joyce, and Karen, I offer my gratitude for helping me maintain space in my mind and body to undertake this task.

To Ethel and Diane and my Light Sisters, thank you for being the mirror. To my special teachers, Joanne, Caroline, Jennifer, and Linda, thank you for the roles you played along my journey.

My agent, Linda Konner, coached me through the proposal stage and offered her lovely brand of magic to match this project with Suzanne Staszak-Silva, my editor at Rowman & Littlefield. I am grateful to both of them for taking on a publishing newbie and shepherding both the book and me through the process with attentiveness and care.

And you, gentle readers, you and your children were in my mind as I wrote this book. Thank you for your willingness to open your hearts to the ideas within and to each other.

INTRODUCTION

Fear is the watershed in adoption. We must come to terms with fear, bring parents over to the brave side of things.
—James L. Gritter[1]

HOW DEEP IS YOUR LOVE?

Ask any mom if she would run into a burning building to rescue her son. Ask any dad if he'd step in front of a careening bus to save his daughter. Ask any set of parents if they would risk coming between a coupon shopper and a Black Friday sale if their child's life depended on it.

You'd get three resounding yeses. Love transcends all, they'd say—even fear.

But ask people if they could fathom inviting their child's birth parents to a birthday party. Ask a mom if she could stay calm as her daughter wonders aloud about living with her birth parents. Ask a dad if he could handle his son's questions about his other set of parents without a tightening in the chest, without shutting down.

You might find that these parents would question their ability to face their fears.

My then-eight-year-old daughter, Tessa, was distraught one October evening at not being allowed to sleep over at her aunt's house. The excitement of trick-or-treating, the disappointment about the sleepover, and a sugar high made for a meltdown.

Once in the car on the way home from a family dinner, she continued to wail about how mean her dad and I are. The wailing about the nixed slumber party changed tone as we headed home.

"Why can't Crystal and Joe be my parents? I have never even been with both of them at the same time!"

Whoa.

Crystal and Joe are Tessa's birth parents.

I silenced the radio so I could focus. Here's a slowdown of my processes during moments like this: calm, center, open. Breathe. Listen. Let her do most of the talking. Assess. What is she really saying or asking? Trade places. What might this look like, feel like, to her? Abide. Give her space to feel her feelings. Speak with equal parts head and heart.

"Tell me more," I said while driving home.

"If they got together, maybe they would *like* each other. And then . . ."

"And then . . . ?" (pause) "And then they could be your parents?"

"Yes." (pause) "But Joe is married, and Crystal has her boyfriend." (pause) "They will never be married, will they, Mom?"

Now, the important thing I did here was not to personalize this and make it about *me*. Tessa's words, and the thoughts behind them, had nothing to do with her feelings for Roger and me, her attachment to us, her love for us. The best way for me to help her find resolution about having two sets of parents and about her own road not taken is not to pretend that one set of parents doesn't exist, is not to feel bad that I can't be everything to her, is not to "fix" it for her by pointing out all she does have.

It's by giving her space and support to find her own way.

Open adoption isn't just something parents do when they exchange photos, send e-mails, share a visit. It's something that can come up even when we have other plans. Openness is the spirit in which we parent, teach, counsel, and listen to our children.

How does an adoptive parent know how to respond in such an unplanned conversation? I am frequently asked questions like this on my blog, *LavenderLuz.com*. This book is, in part, a response to the cry for help over how to enter and navigate the increasingly popular arrangement of open adoption in a child-centered manner and with an open heart.

WHY NOW?

The *Washington Times* reported in 2012 that

> an estimated 95 percent of U.S. infant adoptions now have some level of openness between birth parents and adoptive parents, unlike earlier decades, when such contact was routinely denied. . . . "The era of truly closed adoptions is probably coming to a quick end," said Adam Pertman, executive director of the Donaldson Adoption Institute.[2]

And in the media release for the report Pertman went on to say that

> the good news is that adoption in our country is traveling a road toward greater openness and honesty. . . . But this new reality also brings challenges, and there are still widespread myths and misconceptions about open adoption—so we have a lot of work to do in educating the public, professionals, the media, and the families themselves so that we can continue making progress for the millions of people involved.[3]

WHY *THIS* BOOK?

There are many resources available explaining why to do open adoption, but what about *how*? It's not feasible for any encyclopedia—or even app—to address what do to in every conceivable situation in open adoption. What is possible, however, is create the right mind-set—and heart-set—in which answers can be found, assembled in a guide.

This book does cover the *why* in part 1, laying the foundation for the *how* in part 2. It covers common open-adoption situations and how real families have navigated common issues successfully. Like other useful parenting books, this one provides you with the tools to come to answers on your own.

Part 1, "From Fear to Family: Parents Come Together," addresses the fundamentals of open adoption. It focuses on the two sets of parents in the adoption constellation and answers some important questions:

- What *is* open adoption?
- How do we define a "successful" open adoption?
- What are the emotional benefits and costs of open adoption for parents and for children?
- Why are ethics so important, and how can we ensure an ethical adoption?
- What should birth parents and adoptive parents know when choosing an adoption professional?
- How can we clear our hearts of the grief of infertility in preparation for a child who deserves to be our best choice, if not our first?
- How do we encourage a good match in an open adoption?
- What are the pitfalls that can occur in open adoption?
- What are the ingredients to success in open adoption?

Then part 2, "Orienting on the Child: Open Adoption's True North," focuses on the baby, who becomes a child, then a teen, and eventually becomes an adult, and who is at the center of an adoption. It covers how to create a successful open adoption and incorporate your head and heart to balance the sometimes-competing needs within the adoption triad, as well as how to cultivate openness, even if contact is not possible.[4] Part 2 goes on to address questions that come with the advancing abilities of the child to question and understand her adoptedness:

- The concept of "real" parents
- School assignment: designing an open-adoption family tree
- Search and reunion with a missing birthparent
- Extended birth families
- The push-pull of having another family "out there"
- Pressure to choose or rank parents
- Dealing with the alternate reality, the road not taken, the fantasy life not lived
- The primal wound: the fine line between denying and dwelling on our child's adoption
- When one child has less contact with birthparents than another

- The heartbreak of being questioned or teased by peers
- The role of birth parents in the success of an open adoption
- Our role as ambassadors for open adoption
- Openness in foster adoption, international adoption, and donor-gamete or donor-embryo situations

Whether you are already in or considering entering into a domestic infant adoption, whether you are interested in opening an adoption for your foster child or internationally adopted child, and whether you became a parent through donor sperm, donor eggs, donor embryos, or surrogacy, this book will help you help your child integrate his various selves.

More than a how-to, this book shares a mind-set, a *heart*-set, that can be learned and internalized. This mind-set/heart-set becomes an inner-navigation system that equips you to act confidently from love and not fear.

POWER AND POWER SHIFTS IN OPEN-ADOPTION RELATIONSHIPS

Adoptions in the past were inherently power imbalanced. One set of parents was shamed and minimized, while the other was idealized and legitimized. Open adoptions, however, are created when two sets of parents come together with oddly shaped problems that somehow fit together. Neither is in a superior position, and neither is a supplicant. Instead, there is an inherent equality over time.

Adoption creates a split between a person's biology and biography. Openness in adoption is an effective way to heal that split and help the child become whole.

A BRIEF HISTORY OF OPEN ADOPTION

The state of adoption has changed drastically in the last twenty years. The *Wikipedia* entry on open adoption says that

> until the 1930s, most adoptive parents and biological parents had contact at least during the adoption process. In many cases, adoption

was seen as a social support: young children were adopted out not only to help their parents (by reducing the number of children they had to support) but also to help another family by providing an apprentice.

Adoptions became closed when social pressures mandated that families preserve the myth that they were formed biologically. One researcher has referred to these families, [who] made every attempt to match the child physically to their adoptive families, as "as if" families.[5]

After World War II, when the country was busy repopulating (the Baby Boom), infertility was viewed as shameful, as was pregnancy outside marriage. Thus began the so-called Baby-Scoop Era, in which babies were taken, sometimes forcibly, from unwed mothers and given to infertile couples. Because of the stigma associated with such pregnancies, adoptions during this period, which lasted for many decades, were closed. A biological mother was to keep her secret and forget her baby had ever existed; adoptive parents were to pretend as if the child came to them biologically, and the child was sometimes *never even told* that he was adopted. In addition, birth records were locked up tightly in most states so that the truth would never be known. Adoption was closed, shrouded in darkness, secrecy, and shame.

The enshrouding of adoption began to lift in the 1980s as the social stigma for both unwed mothers and infertile couples began to abate. People began to experiment with openness in adoption, knowing identities of and even having contact with the other parents, having more open discussions among those in the adoption constellation, and sharing birth records with grown adoptees.[6] We find ourselves now moving further into the light, away from the shame. Still, though, many involved in adoption may carry hurt, grief, and loss and perhaps simply don't know how to "do" openness well.

This book shows you how to open your hearts to what is. It will guide you to parenting with an open heart—a vulnerable heart—and help you cultivate a mind-set and heart-set that will in turn aid you in finding answers in the moment to difficult parenting situations. It will show you why you need not be afraid or insecure, and how easy it can be to welcome your child's other parents and family members into your lives. For in doing all this, you are helping your child become whole, embrace all pieces of himself, and to live with an open heart, as well.

A WORD ABOUT THE WORDS

Throughout this book we talk about an *adopting couple* or *adoptive parents*. Even though these terms are plural, we understand and acknowledge that single people adopt as well. But for simplicity's sake, our discussion is in the plural.

And although in many cases both the mother and father are involved in placing their baby for adoption, to simplify we have on occasion used feminine pronouns.

Finally, when speaking about a generic parent or child, we sometimes refer to either *he* or *she*, also for simplification purposes. Please understand in these cases that the concepts are applicable to both genders.

WHO THIS BOOK IS FOR

- People who are hoping to adopt via domestic infant adoption
- Adoptive parents who adopted an infant domestically
- Birth parents who placed an infant domestically, or someone who is considering placing a baby
- People involved in foster adoption—The reasons why openness helps the voluntarily placed child are valid as well for the involuntarily placed child, perhaps even more so. Clearly there may be added layers of complexity in creating an atmosphere of openness, and in some cases safety and boundaries may be a more prominent concern.
- People involved in international adoption who have any chance (or, due to expected building of DNA databases, may have the opportunity in the future) of finding and building a relationship with birth family members—The reasons why openness helps the domestically adopted child hold true (possibly even more, given the change in language, name, culture, and heritage) for the internationally adopted child.[7]
- People involved in donor-gamete conception, including donor sperm, donor egg, and donor embryos—The latest advances in ART (assisted reproductive technology) create ways other than traditional adoption in which the three components of parenting—DNA, preg-

nancy, and raising a child—are split among more than just two people.

- Adoption professionals, including agency counselors, attorneys, facilitators, social workers, and caseworkers—This book supports clients who want to cocreate an open relationship with their child's other parents as well as develop an open-hearted style of adoptive parenting.
- People who are open to exploring openness in adoption, whether or not that means contact

VADE MECUM

As just one of many tour guides you'll have on your journey through the realm of open adoption, I wish you a fulfilling trip that suits you perfectly, that causes you to grow and stretch and become bigger than you are right now. It truly is the journey of a lifetime, yours and your child's. *Vade mecum*—come, go with me.

Part I

From Fear to Family: Parents Come Together

Why open adoption? That's the question we'll focus on in the first four chapters of this book. As a birth parent, why would you want to stay in the life of the child you placed? Why would you subject yourself to the feelings that might emerge when you hear your child call another woman Mama or another man Daddy? As an adoptive parent, why would you complicate your life by having birth parents around—people who have a seemingly competing claim on your child?

The answer is simple: *Adoption creates a split in a person between his biology and his biography. Openness in adoption is an effective way to heal that split.*

But simple doesn't always mean easy. Let's begin part 1 of this book by figuring out just what open adoption is (chapter 1), choosing an ethical adoption professional who can increase your chances for success in openness (chapter 2), getting to know the two sets of parents who come to the open adoption table (chapter 3), and understanding some of the challenges for parents that come with openness (chapter 4).

Later, in part 2, we'll answer the *how* question and address the focal point of all our open adoption efforts—the child. We'll look at the experience of being adopted from both closed and open perspectives (chapter 5). We'll investigate what the process of healing the adoption split looks like for adopted people and for their parents (chapter 6), and we'll examine some parenting challenges that can arise (chapter 7).

We'll take a look at openness in foster, international, and donor situations (chapter 8), and we'll devote a special chapter to birth parents and those who yearn to connect better with them (chapter 9). And then we'll send you on your way, ready to build and sustain a child-centered open adoption that will best help your child grow up whole (chapter 10).

But to start, just what are we talking about when we say *open adoption?*

I

WHAT IS OPEN ADOPTION?

UNCHARTED WATERS[1]

We had a navigation problem with the adoption of our first child. It was as if my husband and I were sailing an inky sea in the velvet night with neither moon nor compass. No guiding star, a little seasickness, and only sheer intuition to go on. We needed to know: Where were we? Where should we go, and on what should we orient? What tools would help us plan our course? Who had been here before, and what experiences did they have?

We'd found ourselves adrift in the Adoption Ocean. Maybe you know the feeling.

HIGH AND DRY

Like many couples, we wanted to build a family. It didn't take long to figure out that we didn't have the required biological building blocks, so we set out to become parents in another way.

Of course, we knew all about adoption—didn't everyone? *We* were to pretend it wasn't adoption, the *biological parents* were to pretend it wasn't adoption, and our future *children* were to pretend it wasn't adoption.

This was the first guiding point that helped us chart our way through the adoption ocean: we soon found out that everything we "knew" was wrong, and we started to see adoption from an entirely new point of view.

Our adoption agency coached us on this newfangled thing called *open adoption*. Not even ten years old at the time, there was very little research available on this alternative to the closed adoptions of the previous five decades. Even now, the children of early open adoptions are just now becoming adults who can express what it was like to have knowledge of and perhaps contact with two sets of parents—one of biology and one of biography.

PERSPECTIVES

When infertility takes away choices, a couple can be struck hard by baby fever. All that matters is having a baby and becoming a parent. When the chosen method is adoption, there can be a myopia that is focused on only one part of the adoption triad—ourselves, the adoptive parents.

But people in successful open adoptions are mindful from the very beginning of the other two parts of the triad—(1) the baby who will become a child, a teen, an adult, and (2) the birth parents who will always have an undeniable influence on the child, no matter the degree of contact.

While some longitudinal research has been done regarding children in open adoption, much of these waters have remained uncharted. Until now.

Using our own experiences and those of others in open adoptions, we'll chart the map for you, let you know where the Bermuda Triangle is, help you avoid murky swamps, fiery volcanoes, and consuming quicksand. And trek the lifelong journey of raising a whole child, one who is able to integrate fully both his biology and his biography.

Before taking up any endeavor, be it sailing or parenting or adoption, you would do well to learn the lingo. So let's first talk terminology, starting with the word *open*.

Does *open* mean exchanging identifying information? Does it mean having contact with birth parents? Does it mean taking family vacations together? Each triad will explore and find answers based on the unique traits and needs of those in it. In this book, *open* refers less to the degree of contact than to the spirit in which we parent and our attitudes about adoption.

Since there is not an academy to define our terms, we will instead attempt to understand how different words are perceived by different people. And while there is no consensus in Adoption World on which terms are acceptable, we know that the words we use both influence and reflect the spirit of our open adoptions. Ultimately you will choose your own, but here are some considerations.

- *Adoptive parent.* Typically, I do not call myself an adoptive mother. I am a mom, period. But in this book, heavy on discussions about both types of parents, I often distinguish this role by calling the forever set of parents the *adoptive parents.*
- *Birth parent or first parent.* There is no definitive answer that ruffles no feathers. But let's explore some commonly used titles.

    - *Birth parents.* This term was coined in the 1970s when Positive Adoption Language emerged, as adoption professionals sought to replace the term *natural parents* with one that didn't indicate that the adopting parents were unnatural. This term is not technically accurate for a father, as he doesn't give birth. And it's too limiting for many mothers— they contribute much more than labor and delivery. They also provide prenatal care and plan as best they can for the child's future. Some dislike it because *birth mother* could imply that the adoptive mother is a *death mother.* Still, it is perhaps the most widely used and understood term currently in use, and it is used throughout this book. I keep it as two words to put it on par with *adoptive parents* (rather than *adoptiveparents*).
    - *Biological mother.* This term limits my children's first parents' role to that of DNA providers. In fact, in my family's case, Crystal and Michele have much more significance than just biology to us. They made decisions during and after their pregnancies that show they are much more than gene donors and incubators. To me, this term is just too clinical, although it is well understood in adoption circles.

- *Real mom.* So, who changed all those diapers and woke up in the middle of all those nights to soothe—Fake Mom? *Real* means *exists*, so this would include both moms or both sets of parents.
- *First parent.* This term honors the people who gave life and does not diminish the role of the adoptive parents. Rather than implying that the adoptive mom is second, it denotes that she is last—forever. However, from a child's perspective, *first* may imply *second* and *third* and so on, with a possible a sense of impermanence. Still, I often use this term as one of honor.

CRYSTAL SAYS: Personally? I like *birth mom*. I gave birth to Tessa. The term includes all that led up to her birth, meaning the prenatal care and all that.

I dislike *real mom*. Lori and I are both real.

I've never claimed *mom* as my title, even though Tessa calls me that once in a while. Lori and I decided to let her figure out the language she wants to use and not correct her as she tries out words. What's the harm in letting her direct this? She knows what's what. The way I see it, the mom is the one who gets up in the middle of the night, the one who holds the hand through teeth cleanings, the one who helps with homework every afternoon. For Tessa, I don't feel that's me. I'm comfortable with being called her birth mom.

Throughout this book you'll see both *birth parent* and *first parent* used interchangeably, as we think they're the best among the terms that are readily understood.

Based on my research with first mothers, I recommend not using *our* before birth/first mom, as in "Our birth mom will visit soon." That's been likened to owning a breeder cow and is technically imprecise—she is not your birth mom; she is your child's birth mom. Instead, say, "Our son's birth mom will visit soon."

And no matter what your intentions, if and when writing about your adoption online, never abbreviate birthmother as *BM*. No one likes to be equated with excrement, even with innocent intentions. Instead, if you are limited on time or keystrokes, try *bmom* or *bdad*, *fmom* or *fdad*.

Please note that these terms are accurate only when referring to parents who have relinquished. Prior to relinquishment, a pregnant woman is simply an expectant mother or mother, no matter what your agency tells you. Use of the term *birth mother*—even when prefixed with the word *prospective*—to describe a pregnant woman who might choose adoption—is considered coercive. It's not until she legally surrenders her role as parent that she should have any prefixes attached to her title at all.

OUR DESTINATION

So where are we headed? Becoming a mom or dad is just the first leg of the journey. Being a child-centered parent—through toddlerhood, through preschool and elementary school and the tween and teen years—*that* is the destination. How do we define success on the journey?

Each adoption triad (first parents, adoptive parents, and the child him- or herself) must decide what success looks like, but here are some considerations from people in open adoptions.

Success might mean that members of your triad give each other permission to feel and express feelings appropriately, even if those feelings aren't pretty. When the adults in the triad do this, we show our children how to do this for themselves—a valuable life skill.

Success might mean setting boundaries out of love rather than out of fear or insecurity. The more both sets of parents resolve their own adoption issues (which may be tied to infertility and/or loss), the fewer the child will have to resolve.

Success might mean leading with your heart as well as with your mind. Being both sensitive and sensible. Being aware and conscious of your own motivations and attempting to intuit and empathize with those of others.

Adoptive parents have said that success means support, especially for the child but also for the parents involved. That success is knowing that the couple didn't build a family merely by welcoming a child but by extending their family beyond just the child. That success means emotional health and stability for each triad member. That success requires respect and communication.

First parents have said that success means the child is happy. That updates, visits, and relationships are ongoing. That no one in the triad feels victimized. That promises are kept. It means an absence of antagonism. That success is in how you navigate the difficulties.

And one adult adoptee has said that success lies in how well the needs and desires of the adoptee are met.

The author of *What to Expect from Your Adopted Teen* (and, believe it or not, your baby will eventually become a teen), Judy M. Miller has this to say about successfully raising an adopted child:

> It's imperative that our children know that we support them and have respect and empathy for their story. This means that we as parents must, when first making the decision to adopt, realize and accept that our parenting journey is truly centered around our child and their best interests, not ours.
>
> We need to examine our feelings about "sharing" with our child their birth parents, history, culture, etc. The good as well as the difficult truths. We do our kids no favors by keeping part or all of their stories from them, and this includes anything in their past. They need as much as we know and can share/expose them to in order to form their identity.
>
> Openness is best, and communication must begin as soon as the child enters the family, whether or not there is birth-parent involvement, in age-appropriate language and concept. Every situation is different; each child's story is unique, and it is the parent's job to encourage their child to explore it, as it is part of her identity. The child who has been adopted may struggle with the need to know and the fear of asking for fear of hurting or "losing" (tied back to the inherent core issue of rejection). Even when your child begins to push you in her tween and teen years, be open, focus on and support her. She needs you; hold her hand, and you will also hold her heart.[2]

Open adoption is a process, not a point in time. It is a direction you aim for. And you periodically check to see if you are still on the desired path. Much like a happy marriage has both good times and challenging times, a successful open adoption will also have ups and downs. The measure is in how the peaks and valleys are handled over the long run.

What does a successful open adoption look like to you?

CRYSTAL SAYS: Trust is probably the most important ingredient for success in our open adoption. Two trust-building things happened the day after Tessa was born, the day we all left the hospital, each of us carrying a different load. This is the first.

Tessa had been born early in the morning the day before. So I had already spent a day and a half with this beautiful, wonderful being. My baby girl. She was so small and precious.

With all the love in me I knew that she was going to have a chance because of the decision I was making.

I had known Lori and Roger for about ten days. We had met once at the agency, once over dinner (my four-year-old son joined us), and once at a get-together with my family. Even though I knew I would be a great mom to my baby girl, as I already was to my son, I also knew in my heart that Roger and Lori were going to be wonderful parents and could give my daughter the stability and security that her birth father and I weren't in a position to give her then.

The morning of the day Tessa and I were to leave the hospital—separately—I was feeling very emotional, which is to be expected. I felt that I needed to call Lori and reassure her that my sadness was exactly what it was: sadness, not me changing my mind.

We had a long telephone conversation before they came back to the hospital. I tried to imagine what they were feeling. And at the same time I was managing my own emotions. I somehow knew it was very important for us to be very upfront with each other. Which meant I had to be very clear with myself.

I told Lori that I was sad. *Big* sad. I told her that I was likely to cry. *Big* cry. And I told her that, in spite of all that, I was still certain that I was doing the best thing for my daughter. I asked her to trust me, even through the tears that would surely come.

With this phone call, we started building our bridge of trust. And the trust building went both ways. This conversation paved the way for what happened next, when Lori and Roger took a trusting leap of faith in me.

Later as we all prepared to leave the hospital, with their new family going one way and me going the opposite direction, home to my mom and my son, Lori and Roger sprang a surprise on me. I had wanted so badly for my grandmother, who was dying of cancer at her home, to see the new baby. But she wasn't well enough to travel to the hospital. Lori and Roger overheard me saying so, and, against all advice they'd been given, they drove Tessa to my grandmother's house. My grandma, my mom, my son, and I all sat on the couch with this newborn miracle. I was so pleased that Lori and Roger came into our home that day and encouraged that moment to happen. When they finally left, I was grief-stricken at the loss of Tessa, but I also knew that we were on the best possible track to build a relationship. At that moment we became connected for life, with Tessa as the reason and trust as our foundation.

DECIDING ON THE DESTINATION: PROS AND CONS

Like most decisions in life, choosing openness in adoption involves trade-offs. Let's take a look at what is gained and what is lost with openness.

Pros	Cons
More people to love you and your child	More relationships; more chances for complications
You have access to your child's medical history as it unfolds in the lives of his birth-family members	Control issues may arise
Your grown child has access to medical history as it emerges (as birth parents age and when issues tend to develop)	As with in-laws, you may have to interact with people you might not ordinarily choose to
The child is less divided in his or her loyalties	Possible boundary issues

The child does not wonder about the *whos* or *whys*; gaps in his or her story can be addressed when the child is ready to ask and process bits of the story

Possible feelings of insecurity for parents

The child has access to people he or she looks like (genetic mirroring)

Fear that the child will be confused

The child has the opportunity to merge his or her biology and his or her biography

Others you would add?

Others you would add?

THE BIRTH OF AN OPEN ADOPTION RELATIONSHIP: LUNA AND MAC

Luna and Mac are parents of a three-year-old. While they did not conceive Jaye, nor did Luna give birth to her, nevertheless Luna and Mac were very busy prior to her birth, getting ready for her and for openness in their adoption.

Luna and Mac, by self-admission, had scars and bruises, both physical and emotional, as they headed into the adoption process. After suffering the indignities and losses inherent in infertility and prenatal loss, they were more than a little incensed at facing more indignities through adoption. *It'll take so long! There are no guarantees! So many risks! We have to prove ourselves worthy of parenthood when fertile people don't!*

First they had to heal from previous losses—a miscarriage and lost hopes—and take that leap of faith into this new possible way of building a family. Through counseling and journaling, they worked through their grief, a process that transforms anger into acceptance, and that may be ongoing. Luna knew she was well on the path to healing with this journal entry:

> It's interesting moving in this new direction. We're moving from hopeless to hopeful, from powerless to becoming empowered. It is

very much a new light. As I've heard from so many others, it feels different. For now, there is forward motion. There are things within our control that must be done—forms to be completed, tough questions to be considered, books to read, support groups to attend.

While we may not be truly prepared for the wait and other uncertainties, it feels in a real sense that we are taking the first true steps toward building our family, when before we were merely spinning in circles or at a standstill. This is positive movement.

I don't think we could have come to this point any other way. Unless the best experts had told me years ago that I had no chance whatsoever of conceiving or carrying a child, I would have done all I could to try. I have no regrets or anger over trying. I believed in the chance. I'm just done failing. I'm ready to reclaim my body and life.

I've already done so much grief work, dealing with infertility and losing our son. I was guided by a professional grief counselor, I did a lot of reading and writing, I leaned into the strong support of a small online community. I continue to reflect on and write about my ongoing process here.

Yet I must keep moving forward. *I am ready to let go.* [3]

The letting go made room. And in the resulting space Luna and Mac were able to begin opening their minds and hearts to new possibilities.

Luna and Mac had heard of open adoption through their network of friends. The openness and expansiveness appealed to them, so they began to explore and learn more about it, including their friends and family in their discoveries.

It was during this exploration that their adoption profile, which was literally hot off the press, had been passed to a friend of a friend who was two months into an unexpected pregnancy. Within days, Luna and Mac were talking to Kaye on the telephone. They met her shortly thereafter. Luna says, "Before we met Kaye, open adoption was still somewhat of an abstraction to us. I had begun to read a lot about it, we had seen the beauty and love in families extended through open adoption, and we continued to educate ourselves. Open adoption made a lot of sense to us for many reasons, and we decided it was something we wanted for our child. Still, until we met Kaye and spent some time together, we weren't really sure how it would work for us. It was a mere concept yet to be applied in practice." [4]

Very early in her pregnancy Kaye selected Luna and Mac to parent her baby. This gave Luna and Mac many months to settle in with all the *what-ifs* that could happen during the pregnancy and after the birth of Kaye's baby. Luna journaled,

> Nearly four months have passed since we first heard about Kaye and her situation. It's been over three months since we met Kaye and she asked us to parent her baby before she was even halfway to term. It seems like not so long ago I was feeling as if the due date would not come soon enough. And now it's just two quick months away.
>
> We've given people permission to be excited, because we are. They can feel cautious too—that's appropriate. But not fearful. The comments that come from a place of fear are troubling to me. I disregard them and find myself doing a little educating too. It's not just about us. It's about this baby and what's best for him/her. It's about Kaye and what's best for her. We don't want people to judge the situation. It's not their place. It is what it is. And this may be our child's story. Tread lightly, people.
>
> When others see that we embrace this possibility with open hearts, there are usually two reactions: love and fear. It's been very interesting to notice this. The love reaction is: *How wonderful, What a beautiful way to build your family*, excitement about the connection, genuine joy, etc. The fear reaction is: *When does she sign, Are you sure you really want to* (insert any thing we're planning), or *I knew someone whose adoption failed*, and *What would you do if* (blah, blah, blah). . . .
>
> If this placement were to fall through and we were crushed, that would be so regardless of how we feel right now. Our heart has already opened to Kaye and to this child. We can't help that. And why should we? As long as we maintain appropriate respect for Kaye and her choices, we have nothing to gain by withholding our hearts (as if that were possible) yet everything still to lose.
>
> A friend likened our approach to holding something wonderful and precious in the palm of your hand. You can marvel and awe at its beauty and nature, you can appreciate how lovely it feels at this very moment. But you can't grasp too tightly, or you will distort it, maybe destroy it. The more tightly you grasp, the more quickly it will slip right through your fingers. . . .
>
> What choice do you have but to stand in awe, or run in fear?[5]

As the due date approached, Luna, Mac, and Kaye chose a tree as a metaphor for their relationship, and together they created a visual symbol of their interconnection.

For a long time, I wavered between embracing the uncertainty and the fear before I could completely let go and flow with this process. Time was relative and distorted, and it seemed we had *so* very long to wait before Kaye's due date.

Yet now, with Kaye at thirty-seven weeks and preparing for labor, we are finally preparing a nursery! And the best part is Kaye joined us this weekend to help create this beautiful space for Baby.

Mac and I really wanted to create something symbolic of our journey and of this child. Because this baby's story is so intertwined with nature, as is our connection to Kaye, it seemed, well, only natural to incorporate a theme around a "tree of life."[6]

The baby's nursery was decorated with a hand-painted family tree. The tree emerged from the minds, hearts, and hands of the baby's mom and two hopeful parents. The tree was sturdy and enduring, with strong roots, reaching branches, lush leaves.

Finally, it was time for the birth.

The most beautiful single moment is one where I saw our daughter being born. Only in a truly open adoption could I have had the privilege to be present and participate in her birth experience as I did.

Jaye was born at home, in her birth mom's home, surrounded by skilled midwives and loved ones. The moment I saw her head slowly emerge, I held my breath in awe. I simply could not believe what we were witnessing. As her tiny body came out, I caught her. (Not many women can say they caught their own child!)

The midwives quickly wrapped warm blankets around the baby as I held her for just a moment before passing her to Kaye. We still didn't yet know whether she was a girl or a boy, and it was my job to call out her gender. But she was covered by the blanket! One of the midwives opened it up so I could see.

"Oh, Kaye! She's a beautiful girl!" I cried, in tears—and to my Mac, "A beautiful girl . . ."

After we hugged, sobbing tears of awe and joy, I looked up and realized there was not a dry eye in the room.

And a new family was born.[7]

Openness with their baby's first mother began successfully for Luna and Mac. They'd had a chance to meet and bond with Kaye, to develop a trusting relationship. Kaye had freely made her decision to place, and she made it again after her baby's birth. Adoption experts acknowledge that the decision is not truly made until after the baby is born.

What about the other side of Jaye's biological family, Jaye's first father? Luna and Mac wanted to open their hearts to him, as well. But before he came into their world, his mother did, Jaye's paternal-birth grandmother. And the road got bumpier.

Any family has its own dynamics, especially with in-laws or grandparents. Yet open adoption brings even more people to the table. Instead of four potential grandparents, there could be eight (or sixteen with stepparents, etc.). That's a lot to negotiate, potentially.

Meeting the paternal first parents was emotionally charged. A first meeting. A brand new baby. A new family. First-time grandparents with little connection to their son and a fear of loss. A safe neutral place. A few hours' time.

Unlike a phone conversation or e-mail, an in-person meeting provides added dimension. A hug, a smile, a firm handshake, the smell of a baby's head or a kiss on her cheek—these are things you can't convey electronically. Yet with this also comes interpretation. Even the slightest comment or gesture can be misconstrued. Eye contact, body language, even clothing, all convey much about who we are and what we intend.

And so it was that we experienced our first meeting with Jaye's biological grandmother, step-grandfather, and young aunt on a hot summer afternoon when Jaye was nearly ten weeks old.

The high points? Putting faces to the names, voices, and stories. Watching Jaye's eleven-year-old aunt feed her a bottle and offer to babysit. Hearing that they are happy with this outcome. Seeing the knitted blanket made for Jaye. Taking photos that she will have forever.

The tough moments? Knowing they will always want and expect more than we are willing to give. Realizing how little the birth grandmother knows about Jaye's biological father—her own son. Hearing a misguided comment about loss inappropriately dumped onto a tiny child. And, finally, what could have been a sweet gesture of pride instead comes across as an improper claim of possession.

When I say "claim of possession," I don't mean proudly referring to Jaye as "ours," or saying, "Look, she's got his chin." It's the belief that a child is a possession to be claimed or owned rather than a little being in need of care, guidance, and connection. The child is viewed as secondary rather than as a unique individual in his or her own right. Ultimately, it's about the person seeking to claim and not about the child. This is a significant issue that any parent should ponder, I think.

For now, any decision regarding the extent or frequency of our future in-person contact is left in the balance. I imagine we will have contact, but clearly we will need to establish some boundaries to preserve and respect our own family unit.

Maybe this is all normal. Relationships such as these can be awkward. Certainly birth grandparents suffer great loss too. I intend to ensure that they know this child in whatever way is possible, mostly for Jaye.[8]

Luna and Mac recognized that open adoption is a journey rather than a destination. There is no *there* there. There is just the getting there. They hope for long-term success, which Mac currently defines as "the joy I feel at watching the smiles on my daughter's and her birth mom's faces when Kaye holds Jaye in her arms."[9]

ON DNA

What's the big deal about biology, anyway? Aren't the adoptive parents the "real" parents, even though the child doesn't share their DNA?

It may be easy to discount a genetic connection once you've gotten on the adoption path. If you're in an either/or mind-set—either *they* are the parents or *we* are—you almost have to downplay biology in order to elevate yourself.

But remember? Likely, you tried very hard at one time to have a biological child. You wanted to gaze into a face that looked somewhat like yours or your beloved's or a glorious combination of both. You wanted to share your lives with someone who shared your traits and had bits of your bioinformation swimming in her veins. Biology probably *was* important to you at one stage of your journey.

For all these reasons biology may also, at points along the way, be important to your child. For a teeny-weeny double helix, DNA sure packs a punch.

When *Who Do You Think You Are?* debuted on NBC, a couple of my blog's readers asked what I thought about how one's DNA answers the question *Who are you?*—especially in light of adoption.

I'm not a genealogist, but I do enjoy looking at old photo albums that belonged to my grandparents and that feature their parents. The generation of my great-grandparents goes back to the 1880s, and we don't have any photographs from before that time.

I enjoy the stories of my maternal Scotch-Irish grandfather, who grew up in a sod house in Nebraska, a twin and one of nine children. I mourn that I don't know much about my Jewish paternal grandmother's history, other than the fact that her father owned a shoe store in Manhattan. She converted to Catholicism before my dad was born, and her Jewishness was hidden from us until a decade before her death. I missed out on knowing about some of my heritage.

When you think about it, isn't it amazing to contemplate a thread that goes back farther than your mind can grasp? That there is an unbroken line from you stretching to the dawn of humankind? That line, and the relationship webs that accompany it, connects each of us to every person who has ever taken a breath on this planet.

Teeny-weeny DNA makes me think gigantic thoughts like that.

DNA and the role of genetics can weigh even more heavily on people involved in adoption. Adoptees grow up with the biology of one clan and the biography of another and are sometimes unsupported in healing that split. Adoptive parents must accept that they have no hereditary influence on their child. Birth parents may grapple with the idea that a child of their own genetic line was lost to them.

So the question is, do I like poring over those musty photo albums because the people in them are part of my genetic line? Or do I like poring over those musty photo albums because I can see the people who raised the people who raised me?

It's probably both. Nature *and* nurture both play a role in my fascination with my roots.

I don't have to put nature and nurture in a hierarchy, because in my case they are the same. But people who were adopted are often prompted to rank their influences. *Who made you more of who you are—your adoptive parents or your birth parents?* an inquisitor might pry. In asking the question that can't be answered, there is no win, only loss, because the question itself emphasizes and reinforces the split.

Why can't we simply acknowledge that both biology and biography are important? Why don't we move from either/or thinking to and/both thinking? I'm not even talking about fifty-fifty or equal measures, be-cause some things cannot be put on a scale.

I'm just saying that DNA matters. And as a mom via adoption, that doesn't bother me at all. Because I matter, too.

STEPPING FORWARD

The journey begins with the first step. And, for many, that step involves exploring adoption professionals. In the next chapter, we'll take a look at how to choose wisely.

2

WHAT TO CONSIDER WHEN CHOOSING AN AGENCY OR ADOPTION PROFESSIONAL

Just as you want peace of mind that your airplane is piloted by a captain who has what it takes to get you from point A to point B, when you embark on an adoption journey you'll want the same from your adoption professional. But unlike the world of aviation, there is no FAA equivalent to make sure minimum requirements are met. The world of adoption has been called the Wild, Wild West, and wise adopting and expectant parents will need to research the key people who will help them get from where they are to where they want to be. It is, as we've said before, the trip of a lifetime—the child's.

I remember starting my own journey. All I wanted to know at the time was how much the adoption would cost and how long we would have to wait. As I called a bunch of agencies in our city, I had my eyes mostly on the short-term goal of becoming parents. I figured ethics was a given in any agency, right? If the good State of Colorado had put its seal of approval on it, surely an agency would do everything with the highest of morals. Right?

Not necessarily so. It was later that I realized I should also have been asking deeper, more subtle questions that would protect our children and their birth parents (and therefore us!) over the long run. My husband and I got lucky and ended up with an ethical agency, but I admit it was through no due diligence on my part. Other preadoptive parents and expectant parents have not been so fortunate.

WHY YOU NEED AN ADOPTION PROFESSIONAL

Before we get into ethics, let's talk about the tasks that you need an adoption professional to perform and the three types of adoption professionals that exist today.

There are three main duties that adopting parents may need from an adoption professional:

1. *Someone to perform the home study.* In all states this must be a licensed social worker who meets the requirements of your home state.
2. *Someone to help match with an expectant or birth parent.* In some states an adopting couple is legally able to find their own match. This is called a *designated* or an *identified* adoption.
3. *An attorney to handle the legal aspects of becoming the child's parents.* This becomes especially complicated if more than one state is involved in the adoption.

And although in some states it's not legally required, you'll also want to consider having grief counseling available to you to deal with any residual trauma from infertility, as well as for counseling during preplacement, the placement process, and postplacement.

Furthermore, a good adoption professional can help you

- vent your grief so that a baby comes into your home as the best choice, if not the first
- identify and deal with red flags and warning signs that may arise between the time you're matched with an expectant mom and the time she relinquishes
- get on your feet as a new parent
- deal with postadoption depression syndrome (should it manifest)
- and facilitate later interactions with birth family members.

By comparison, the requirements for what placing parents need a professional to do on their behalf are minimal:

- *Counseling about her options.* Any woman considering placing her child for adoption should be presented in detail all other options available to her—especially the option to parent her child herself. If she is looking at adoption primarily for economic reasons, which can be temporary, her pregnancy counselor should present her with all of the resources available to support her in parenting. It is only with this information that the mother can come to the decision to place freely and with the least amount of regret later. Why is this in the best interest of the adopting parents? Because it's so much easier to have an open adoption with birth parents who freely chose adoption as the best of their available options.

Further, there will likely be enormous grief for the mother to process during and after placement. Ideally, an adoption professional will be there to prepare her for it, hold her hand during it, and help her through it—even years later if necessary.

- *Advocacy.* Many in the field advise—and some states require—that the placing parent have her own counselor, separate from the adopting parents' counselor. There's a reason that a home buyer and a home seller have different agents—so that each party has someone in the know with their best interests in mind. Similarly, an expectant parent should have someone experienced in placement who can alert her to warning signs in the adoption process, advise her about both short-term challenges and the effects of placement on the rest of her life, and advocate on her behalf when necessary.
- *Legal representation.* In all fifty states, placing parents sign away their legal rights as parents. Some states also require placing parents to go before a judge to answer a few brief questions clarifying whether they understand their actions and the ramifications of their decisions. The ethical choice, again, is for the placing parents to have different legal representation than the adoptive parents have so that there are no conflicts of interest in the professional advice offered.

THREE TYPES OF ADOPTION PROFESSIONALS

So what are your choices in piloting your adoption? Laws differ from state to state, but three main types of adoption professionals are common.[1]

1. *Agency.* An adoption agency is licensed to place children in adoptive homes by the state (or states) in which it operates. An agency can be either *public*, funded by the state or other government entity, or *private*, funded by client fees and/or donations.[2] A private agency can be either *for-profit*, in which the profits are distributed to shareholders/owner(s) after expenses are paid, or *not-for-profit*, in which funds left after covering expenses are put back into the agency's operations. Be careful about assuming that one is better than the other. Laura Beauvais-Godwin and Raymond Godwin state in *The Complete Adoption Book: Everything You Need to Know to Adopt a Child* that you ought to "remember, just because an agency is incorporated as a nonprofit entity does not mean that the owner of the agency is not profiting from the organization; the owner will profit by drawing a salary. Nor does another agency's for-profit status imply that those who operate the agency are money-hungry and unscrupulous."[3]

   An agency can do either or both of the tasks an adopting person needs them to do: complete the home study, which enables it to legally place a child, and/or match an adopting client with a placing mother.

   Some states require that all adoptions be handled by a licensed adoption agency. Check with the laws in your state to find out what your options are.

2. *Facilitator.* Think of the adoption facilitator as a matchmaker. Some states allow for nonagency intermediaries to bring together, for a fee, a couple or single who hopes to adopt with a mother or couple seeking to place. The practice of using an adoption facilitator or attorney is called arranging for a *private adoption* or *independent adoption.*

   Some states that allow use of a facilitator do not require licensing or regulation. Using an unlicensed or unregulated facilitator can thus be riskier than using a licensed agency, both in financial and legal risk. Another drawback to using a facilitator is that facilitators often provide no preplacement counseling or postadoption support to either the adopting couple or to the expectant couple. In addition, the home study still needs to be performed by a licensed social worker approved by the state.

3. *Attorney.* Like a facilitator, in some states an adoption attorney may also play the matchmaker role. And also like a facilitator, an attorney is not qualified to perform a home study. Unlike a facilitator, however, an attorney has the legal expertise and standing to draw up documents and execute them on behalf of clients. Not all states authorize the use of attorneys for adoption placements.

There is a key difference in placement between using an attorney and using an agency. With an agency, a placing parent relinquishes parental rights to the agency first, which then legally transfers parental rights to the adopting parents after a period of postplacement supervision. When using an attorney, the placing parents transfer legal rights directly to the adopting parents.

In most cases, if you are working with a licensed agency it will guide all involved parties through the required legal steps: (1) identification and notification of the birth father, (2) termination of birth-parent rights, and (3) possibly even finalization of the adoption. If you choose to work with a facilitator, you will also need an attorney or agency to assist with all legal issues of the placement. Some people also use an attorney to find a match. There can be the same limitations and risks in doing so that there are in using a facilitator— there will quite possibly be no counseling for either expectant or adopting parents, an attorney is not qualified to perform a home study, an attorney's fees are likely high, and no postplacement support for either party is possible.

For both of our adoptions, our chosen agency shepherded us through home study, matching, and all legalities for us and our children's birth parents (we had different advocates within the agency, however). We did have an adoption attorney represent us as we appeared before a judge at finalization, though we could have done the filing part ourselves had we wished to figure out the ins and outs of adoption filing. In some cases, the adoption agency has an attorney who will handle the legalities on the clients' behalf.[4]

LET'S START AT THE VERY BEGINNING: THE LOGISTICS OF AN OPEN-ADOPTION RELATIONSHIP

Crystal and I have an unsurprising bias: if you are set on your child reaping the benefits of openness, which you'll understand more fully as you read this book, consider selecting your adoption professional locally (though we know that there are other factors you may incorporate into your decision making). Why? Because then the child's other parents are more likely to live near you, making it easier for all of you to build an extended family relationship from the very beginning of your child's life. The logistics of maintaining meaningful relationships as your child grows up are easier the closer you live to one another (understanding that circumstances change and people sometime move). As you'll see in coming chapters, the daughter Crystal and I both claim has enjoyed having both of us present at her dance recitals, birthday parties, grade-level graduations, choir concerts, and other milestones.

And if this sounds like just too much openness for you to bear, you may find a shift in your thinking by the time you finish reading this book.

DESPERATE PEOPLE + BEAUCOUP BUCKS = HIGH RISK FOR AN ETHICAL LAPSE

Take one couple (or single person) desperate for a baby, add in another couple (or pregnant mom) in a dire situation, then require that a large sum of money change hands to yet a third party. Might that be a recipe for something shady or even combustible? To temper this volatile mix you'll want to ensure a high standard of ethics for the intervening agency, facilitator, or attorney.

Every adoption has three constituents, and the parental ones (adoptive parents and birth parents) should aim to be mindful of the needs and perspectives of the others in the constellation. First there is the adopting couple, the ones who pay the fees and, perhaps (if you're like I was), feeling some measure of baby lust. Then there is the mother or couple in an unexpected pregnancy, needing services but often without the means to pay for them. Finally, the last constituent is the one that everyone else says they're all about—the baby. Who, because he is "just" a baby (perhaps not even born yet), is often seen as a tabula rasa, a blank slate, a hypothetical human being, the voiceless and choiceless one. Regarding the baby, it's been said that there are two types of adoption professionals: (1) one type aims to find a child for a home; (2) the ethical type is concerned with finding a home for a child. Can you understand what the difference might be, from a child's perspective? From a placing parent's perspective?

What questions should adopting parents ask when researching adoption-service providers? And how does a pregnant woman who is looking into adoption discern an ethical professional from a nonethical one? Let's break it down for both sides.

QUESTIONS TO ASK THE ADOPTION PROFESSIONAL

Of course hopeful adopting people want to know how long and how much. But there's so much more that should be delved into. Note that with the discussion questions below, in most cases there are no right or wrong answers. The responses that come from the questions you ask should help you develop a sense of the people you are interviewing and enable you to compare them with each other. Some of these questions apply only to those adopting, but many can also be asked by those placing.

- *What type of adoption professional are you?* You want to determine if you're dealing with a licensed agency, a licensed facilitator, an unlicensed facilitator, or an attorney. Find out what services are provided: home study, matching, counseling, legal tasks? Discern which services, if any, would be outsourced by this provider and whether you will pay separately for that outsourcing.

- *What is a typical wait?* This is just an ice-breaker question. Many professionals will tell you there is no typical wait, that there are so many variables and such a wide range. If you are told a short typical wait, say less than six months as an average, you might see a red flag, warning you that perhaps you are simply being told what you want to hear.

- *What's the shortest wait you've had? What made it so short?* It doesn't hurt to find out what has worked for other waiting families.

- *What's the longest wait? Why do you think this person/couple waited so long? What did you do to help them?* Again, you're mining this provider for what works and what doesn't, as well as finding out what support it offers.

- *How many placements did you have last year?* This number has meaning only in context with other numbers. If it's too high for the number of expectant women who came in the door, there could be subtle coercion of pregnant women going on. If it's low in relation to the number of waiting families, your wait may be long.

- *What percentage of pregnant women who come here end up placing?* Higher is not necessarily better, as it can indicate pressure to relinquish. There is not an agency standard, so rather than a number, what you're looking for with this question is what level of respect an expectant mother is accorded by this adoption professional.

- *How many couples/singles do you have active at any one time?* Our agency aimed to keep twenty couples in The Book (a collection of active adoption profiles) at a time so that placing mothers had enough to choose from, but not so many that the waits were long for hopeful couples. Like many of these measures, it's a fine balance, and it has meaning only in relation to other numbers.

- *Please explain your fee schedule.* A significant portion, up to one-third of the total, should be due at placement.

- *Where does the money go from your fees?* Ask if it's possible to see a financial statement from the previous year, or see if one is available online as part of an annual report. If the entity is concerned with finding a child for a home, you'll see more of its fees go toward marketing. If, on the other hand, the professional aims to find a home for a child, you'll see more of your fees go into counseling. Of course, both are necessary in a proper proportion—you're trying to see if the professional's values match your own.

- *What counseling for us is included in your fees?* Look for grief counseling to heal any residual infertility issues you may have. Such counseling doesn't need to be extensive (it could simply be a referral to a provider), but it should at least be acknowledged that infertility may have left a mark and that a baby deserves to enter a home that has had the grief aired out of it. Also find out if there are postplacement services available to you and to the placing parents.

- *How do expectant parents find you?* While there are no "right" answers to this, you want an adoption professional who walks the line between invisible and aggressive. Having an ad that comes up when someone searches the Internet for "I'm pregnant and need an adoption agency" is possibly okay, but understand that this is marketing and could be evidence that an adoption service provider willing to pay for top-of-the-search results may be more interested in finding a child for a home than the other way around. Trawling online forums for pregnant women and asking if they would place is not okay! (This actually happens, believe it or not.)

- *What is your counseling approach for expectant parents?* When a pregnant woman approaches an agency for counseling, she should be guided to look at all her options, especially parenting the child. Information on resources for parenting should be easily available, and the adoption professional should never push toward a decision but rather provide information and support. Why is this important for the adopting couple or single? It's in your own best interest to ensure that all options have been explored so that there is less regret and chance for reversing the decision later in the process. For the best outcome in openness, the placing mother and father must come to the decision to place freely and as the best of their available options.

- *At what stage of the pregnancy do you suggest expectant parents choose adoptive parents?* Many professionals suggest not entering a match until at least six months into the pregnancy. Expectant parents go through a lot of ups and downs, and you may not want to be riding that roller coaster for too long.

- *How long after placement do you offer counseling and supportive services for birth parents? Does this include birth fathers? And is such counseling included in the adoption fees?* You may find that one professional is more inclusive and attuned to ongoing needs of birth families than another.

- *Describe your postplacement support for adoptive families. And for birth families.* As relationships develop and as circumstances change, it's possible that one or both parties might need help in the future. For example, my daughter's birth father came into our lives when our daughter was six years old. We called on our agency to facilitate this important first meeting with him, which it did for no extra fee.

- *What do you think about open adoption?* Open adoption has been on the rise since the early 1990s, and research indicates that it tends to lead to increased psychological health for both birth parents and adoptees without a negative effect on the adoptive parents.[5] You are looking for a consistency of beliefs and policies, as well as a viewpoint that is expansive enough to include your own. A professional who advises you to talk the talk but not worry about walking the walk is not ethical (there are accounts by adoptive parents of agencies saying, "Go ahead and promise openness to the birth mom. Once it's all finalized, though, you can do whatever you want.")

- *Tell me about the PACAs (postadoption contact agreements).* Find out if your state requires one, how it is enforced, and if the professional will help you draft one. We'll discuss open-adoption agreements in greater detail in chapter 4.

MORE FACT-FINDING FOR YOUR ANALYTICAL SIDE

Here are a few more strategies for researching a professional. First, conduct an Internet search on any person or organization you're considering in order to find out what past clients have said about them. Factor into your decision whatever you discover online. Second, after you have narrowed down your options to a few adoption professionals, visit them in person if proximity permits. Attend an orientation session if offered (during which you might meet past clients, who are often invited), or take advantage of a free consultation. Pay attention to how you feel in this person's space, in this person's presence, and explore any unsettled feelings that come up. Do you need to ask more questions or gain some clarity around a certain issue?

Lastly, ask the professional if you may contact past clients on both sides of adoptions. Listen to the adoptive and birth parents who have used its services and see if their reflection of the entity matches what the provider has told you. Ask the birth parents how they found the agency or facilitator. Ask the birth and adoptive parents if they would recommend this professional to a friend in their same situation. Ask also what kind of relationship the adoptive family and the birth family have with each other, just to see if openness tends to grow in the atmosphere this professional provides for its clients.

Ultimately, what you're looking for are healthy situations in which both parties feel well served and well represented. A good adoption professional will make the adoption process collaborative, with the child as the focus, rather than adversarial, in which one side's loss is the other's gain. An ethical adoption professional is concerned with finding a home for a child and not a child for a home.

BRINGING YOUR HEART INTO THE DECISION

After you gather the facts and build your spreadsheets (if you're like me) to compare your collected data, let your heart weigh in on this momentous decision. Sit quietly, focusing on your heart or your gut, and let your intuition speak to you. If you or your partner has a "feeling" about a professional, go with that feeling. Adoption—like parenting—is a very intuitive process. And so adopting with your head and heart will prepare you to parent with your head and heart.

Needless to say, choosing an adoption agency is one of the biggest decisions you will face in this entire process, because you need to go where your child will be. Engaging both your head and your heart is a good way to make sure your paths will eventually intersect.

CRYSTAL SAYS: When I first began considering adoption, I went to the Yellow Pages (remember those?) and began to proceed with an adoption company that wanted to ship me from Colorado to California for the duration of my pregnancy. They'd put me up in an apartment, buy my food, and pay all my expenses. I'd be a queen! The problem was, the company wouldn't allow my four-year-old son to come with me. Besides that major issue, my intuition was yelling at me to run away fast.

I still knew I needed to place my baby for reasons involving its well-being and mine, as well as my son's. By sheer luck, my grandfather gave me the business card for a nonprofit agency that had been around for more than half a century. He knew of Lutheran Family Services through a friend. I called and got a good feeling about the agency, so I went in for a meeting with them even though I'm not Lutheran. This agency cared more about me as a person than the first place did, where I'd been treated more like a valuable incubator (I later found out it was a facilitator, one that paid big bucks for advertising). At Lutheran, instead, I was offered counseling, much of it having nothing to do with the baby and everything to do with how my life had gotten where it had. The agency didn't push me into placing but followed my lead. In fact, my counselor kept me from looking at The Book of waiting couples until I was nearing my ninth month of pregnancy because she wanted to make sure I'd carefully considered all my options.

Shortly after that, my counselor facilitated my first meeting with Lori and Roger, who were my second choice from The Book (more on that soon). And, once again, my intuition served me well. I knew from that first meeting that this was going to be okay. For all of us.

I'm so glad I tuned in to my inner voice at each turn.

HOT-BUTTON ETHICAL ISSUES

Throughout the adoption process, adopting couples are faced with value judgments that people who become parents in the usual way may never need to face: What are our values regarding race? How do we feel about a child being born with a range of possible disabilities? What issues come up for us regarding the lack of control we have during the gestational time of the child we hope to parent?

These are private decisions that adopting people must clarify for themselves, and the only "right" answer is the one that is in line with their examined beliefs. Integration of values and actions is what you want to achieve.

But aside from these difficult questions, there are even more considerations that may require soul searching. Let's take a look at two ethical issues that you may be faced with as a prospective adoptive parent.

Issue #1: Prebirth Expenses

The term *prebirth expenses* refers to the expectant mother's living or medical expenses that are covered by the adoptive parents during the pregnancy and through the birth, possibly even after placement. This practice can be ripe for ethical lapses. For this reason, many states don't allow it at all, and others allow it only with court approval.[6] Make sure you know what is lawful in your state.

No matter how well it is arranged, when the adopting parents pay expenses for the expecting parents, a sense of indebtedness is created. Remember earlier when we said that open adoptions are created when two sets of parents come together with oddly shaped problems that somehow fit together, and that neither party is in a superior position nor a supplicant, but instead, there is an inherent equality over time? Well, when one side pays expenses for the other side, things get lopsided.

No longer is the situation just about the baby. Now is it also about money, about owing or being owed. And with the central issue clouded, it becomes much more difficult for the expectant mother, especially, to find clarity about her decision whether or not to place.

While such a practice can obscure and distort the situation for the placing mother, it also exposes the adopting couple to financial risk.

Building a long-term trusting relationship can become more difficult when money is involved. As one adopting mom said, "Our adoption agency was very clear in saying that we should not pay for their expenses because it would set up a relationship dynamic that would undoubtedly only get worse."[7]

We've found that some of the most vocal people opposed to the practice of adopting couples paying prebirth expenses are birth mothers themselves. Says Claudia Corrigan D'Arcy, a first mother who has reunited with her son and an activist for adoption reform,

> when coming from the adoptive parents, financial help does add to that sense of obligation felt by the maternity client. On top of their emotional happiness that she holds by either relinquishing or not, having her expenses paid adds another thing she "owes" either them or the agency. In my case, I was emotionally attached to the agency and wanted *them* to be proud of me. Payments made by the adopting parents become another insurmountable issue the mother must face should she decide to parent—*How am I going to pay them back?!*
>
> Here's another thing to consider: how would the expectant mom be paying her living expenses if she *weren't* pregnant?[8]

To further this point, one adult adoptee says, "Honestly? If it had happened in my case I'd feel as if I were bought. I know that's not the intent. And I know there are a lot of great adoptive parents out there who do pay for things. But when it comes down to it, when I learned about the money in adoption for the first time, it made me feel sick that my parents were my parents because they had the money to be."[9]

Brandy Hagelstein, adult adoptee and a birth mother in an open adoption, reveals that the practice of prebirth expenses can also be a red flag for an ethical lapse on the part of the adoption professional.

> [As a placing mother] I never requested expenses. I had very few. I wore sweat pants and T-shirts to class and to work. I had medical care through my insurance and didn't qualify for Medicaid due to my income. But that didn't keep the agency I used from billing the adoptive family for "expenses"—which we discovered several years later. My daughter's parents paid the agency for clothing, food, housing, and counseling—none of which I ever asked for or received. I am not the only birth mother who has experienced this. Two differ-

ent types of professionals were in cahoots on this (mine was a faith-based nonprofit, hers an adoption facilitator).[10]

Ellen Roseman, an adoption facilitator in San Anselmo, California, says that "anyone needing or wanting a large sum of money is turned away from me. But many couples are willing to purchase a baby. Baby purchases and open adoption don't go hand in hand, by the way."[11]

Whenever possible, an adoption agency (or someone advocating for the expectant mom) should provide guidance for the pregnant mother to find housing, food, clothing, and medical assistance independent of the adopting couple. Many agencies use monies from their home-study and placement fees to offer such guidance. And some nonprofit agencies may also have funds available for the actual assistance, coming from donors rather than from clients.

But like so many issues in adoption, there are shades of gray. For example, the planned adoption may be a kinship adoption, meaning that the placing and adopting couples are related in some way. In such a case, assistance is not merely on account of the adoption but also because of family ties. Or there may be a pregnancy-related health concern that keeps an expectant mother from being able to work. Perhaps the expectant mom does not need living expenses but simply needs maternity clothes. Maybe no medical subsidy is available to the pregnant mom, and for the sake of her health and her baby's the adopting parents want to step up and help with prenatal medical bills.

Ellen Roseman has seen hundreds of stories unfold in her decades as a facilitator. She offers some of her best practices regarding prebirth expenses.

> The first rule is not to support a mother prior to the last trimester of her pregnancy. Many in this field will support someone the entire pregnancy if state laws permit. Some states require that money requests go before a judge.
>
> The second rule is to meet prior to any support exchanging hands. Sending money without meeting is risky.
>
> Thirdly, pay expenses from a trust [or fiduciary agency]. The adoptive couple is not to be allowed to discuss money and negotiate this. The rent is paid to the landlord, and other bills are paid directly to vendors. Don't just send someone a pile of money.[12]

Should the issue of paying birth-parent expenses become a decision you face in your adoption process, once again do your due diligence in determining the pros and cons of the practice in general and in your particular situation. Be sure you are following the laws regarding payment of expenses in your state, the birth parents' state, and in whichever state you plan to finalize the adoption. If two or more states are involved, make sure you are not violating laws that would interfere with the Interstate Compact on the Placement of Children (ICPC).

Sit with the facts you gather, and let your heart have its say. Are you able to be honest with yourself about your motives? Can you offer the money with no sense of expectation? If your future child one day asks you about your decision, will your conscience be clear?

To illustrate shades of gray in this issue Robyn shares two different scenarios, one for each of her children, surrounding prebirth expenses.

We adopted my son in January 2006. When we signed with a facilitator the year before, we were given an application on which we stated how much we would be willing to pay in "birthmother expenses." We were told that we could put $0, but that "most girls needed something." The most we could stand to lose was $1,000, so we put that down. At the time, we never thought about the ethics of birthmother expenses, just the risk to us. It seemed like birthmother expenses were a given, and either we could afford to risk them or not.

Our son's birth mother, Sarah, did not initially want anything, not even maternity clothes (she wore her stepfather's sweats). Less than a week before Christmas, she called. She was living in a hotel room with her son, mother, stepfather, and sister. Only her mother was working. They didn't have enough money for the room and were about to be thrown out. Would we mind paying for it? She said she'd pay us back. I told her that we'd check with the attorney, and if it was legal we'd be happy to help and that she didn't have to pay us back. I think it was $300. Due to the way the hospital mismanaged her labor, Sarah had an emergency C-section. The doctor didn't want her to be on her feet more than necessary for six weeks. We paid two more months for the hotel room. Of all of the expenses involved in our son's adoption, those were the ones I least minded paying. She had just made us parents. We could make sure she didn't end up on the street.

Our facilitator was no help at all. Our attorney simply told us what was legal. I don't feel like the money changed our relationship, but maybe it did in Sarah's eyes.

The second time around I was much more aware of the ethical concerns with prebirth expenses. My opinion is that some prebirth expenses are understandable. I don't see a need to pay all of a woman's expenses, but I can see the need to pay some of them. We again had a certain amount that we were willing to risk. This time, however, we were more concerned with what we'd be paying for. We didn't want someone to feel beholden to us.

We lost $1,100 in two matches that didn't pan out. In the first, the mom changed her mind about placing, and in the second we were scammed by someone who likely wasn't even pregnant.

That brings us to our third match, which was with a woman in Louisiana. The facilitator listed the possible expenses, which were within our budget and weren't ludicrous, and also said that these were requests, not demands.

Our daughter's birthmother never asked us for anything other than minutes for her prepaid phone, about $25. But contrary to what the facilitator told us, our attorney then said that when we matched we agreed to pay $1,700 in birthmother expenses (Louisiana is pretty lax about what constitutes "birthmother expenses"), so that's what we would be giving her. In addition, if we wanted to round up and make it $2,000, that would be good.

Our daughter's birth mother didn't have any expenses associated with being pregnant or with delivery. She didn't pay rent, utilities, and the like, because she lived with her father. They both receive assistance from the state. This wasn't like Sarah, who had a C-section and couldn't work. I do know that some money went toward maternity clothes. Other than that, I really feel like we were being asked to pay for her baby.

When I told the attorney that we'd stick with the original number, he tried to guilt us into paying more. Then he argued, "What if she won't sign the papers unless you give her money?" I replied that this was tantamount to buying a baby and he backpedaled a bit. The signing happened. No one mentioned anything more about birthmother expenses.[13]

I asked Robyn to reflect on what might have made the issue of paying prebirth expenses less murky and questionable.

I'd limit expenses to actual expenses. Not, "Well, the state allows $X, so you should give her $X." And unless the expectant mom was on bed rest or had to leave her home for her own safety, I'd greatly limit what counts as a pregnancy-related expense. How would a woman pay rent and utilities if she weren't planning on placing? I could see food being a pregnancy-related expense, as well as a certain allowance for maternity clothing. Medical expenses, counseling, even travel to and from the doctor or hospital. But it really seems that "birth-mother expenses" is a catchall, and it can make a person feel as though she's paying for a baby.

I'd advise a prospective adoptive parent to really think about the ethics of prebirth expenses, beyond just "What are we willing to risk?" Ultimately, they have to decide what they think is best for the situation at hand.[14]

Issue #2: Birth-Father Rights

We sometimes forget that there's a male involved in placing a baby for adoption. After all, it's nearly impossible to consider an adoption without an expectant mom. But too often, adoptions are arranged without the involvement or even permission of the expectant father. The fact that he does not gestate should not minimize his genetic connection to the child or his legal right to be part of the placement decision.

Facilitator Ellen Roseman says it simply: "Best practice is to include birth fathers sooner rather than later."[15] Not only is it the right and honorable thing to do, it's also the expedient thing to do. Finding out about a father late in the adoption process is good for no one.

You can tell a lot about an agency, facilitator, or adoption attorney by what its representatives say about the father of the baby. Claudia Corrigan D'Arcy asks, "Do they reassure the young mother-to-be that he 'won't be an issue' and they 'know how to handle him'? Do they explain that if he wants to parent then he has the right to? Or is he made to sound like a minor irritation?"[16]

In 2009 a woman from Virginia placed her baby for adoption without the consent of the baby's father, John. Upon the birth of baby Emma in a Virginia hospital, John hired an attorney to seek custody in his state, following the rules by putting himself on Virginia's putative-father registry. In Virginia his rights as father were acknowledged by the court.

But little did John and his attorney know that Emma and her mother had been whisked away from the hospital, which would have devastating consequences for John's legal rights. You see, in Utah the father has only twenty days from the baby's birth to get on a putative-father registry. By the time John learned where his daughter was, his time had already expired. In 2011, Utah's Supreme Court ruled against John, reasoning *not* that it was in the best interest of his daughter that she remain with her adoptive parents but that John had failed to exercise his parental rights.[17]

There were many judgment lapses in this story: The birth mother reportedly led John to believe they would raise their daughter together, yet she then went on to make a unilateral decision to place. Legally, that decision should not have been made unilaterally, as in their home state of Virginia John had parental rights to Emma. The agency that the birth mother used may have known how to avoid facing the laws of one state and then possibly may have facilitated a direct-from-the-hospital move to a more adoptive family–friendly state. There, an adoption attorney fought John's stated intent at every turn. Whether Emma's adoptive parents knew anything about the deception or not, it's important that all adoptive parents fully understand what kinds of methods their agencies employ to insure a legal, fair, and safe adoption for all parties involved, including the biological father. Just as adoptive parents would not want to relinquish their parental rights once an adoption has taken place, neither does every biological father wish to relinquish his parental rights simply because his baby's mother decides to take that route. To avoid legal pitfalls, it's important that all parties be in agreement regarding placement.

This story feels very different depending on which role you play in it. If you are John, how would you feel to have lost your child through a miscarriage of justice? If you are the birth mother, how would you carry around the weight of the results of your actions? If you are the adoptive parents, even though you got what you wanted most, wouldn't your joy be alloyed knowing that you had compromised the means to get to your desired end? If you are Emma, how would it feel to know that the people you know as your parents may have been complicit in taking you away from your father who wanted to raise you? If you are the adoption agency or attorney, well, you may have no feelings about this at all.

It is in your own long-term best interest to make sure, whenever possible, that the father of the baby you want to adopt is identified and consents to the adoption.

TIME TO TAXI DOWN THE RUNWAY

So you've found your pilot, and you're headed to your destination: creating and sustaining a child-centered open-adoption relationship. You realize now the importance of ethics and of doing your due diligence, and you understand the lasting effects your choices at this stage will have.

In the next chapter, we'll take a look at how placing and adopting parents come together. So keep those seat belts fastened, because with such a range of people involved, emotions could get a bit turbulent, even on an otherwise smooth ride.

3

THE PARENTS IN AN OPEN ADOPTION

Adoption takes place because of the grownups.[1] Adults (and sometimes adolescents) come together with dissimilar problems that just might complement each other and contribute to resolution. Adopting couples and expectant couples come to adoption with vastly different circumstances and differing degrees of readiness and ability to parent.

A child in adoption has two sets of parents: the set of biology (birth parents) and the set of biography (adoptive parents). How in the world can there be common ground between two groups with opposite problems?

In this chapter we'll address the baggage that each set of parents brings to the open-adoption table. We'll look at the usual path that brings adopting parents here as well as at the burdens weighing them down. We'll get insight from first parents on why placements happen, how decisions are made, and what hopes and dreams they have for the best possible outcome for themselves and for their child.

We'll discuss the tool that often brings the two sets of parents together—the adoption profile—and ways to heighten its effectiveness in sparking the very beginnings of an open relationship. Finally, we'll examine the practice of prebirth matching, looking at two sides of the issue.

NOOKS AND CRANNIES

Crystal and I met because we each had a problem. Mine had nooks with crannies, and hers had crannies with nooks. Our oddly shaped problems fit together, and we became each other's solution.

In 2001 I was five years into the famine that is infertility. At that same time Crystal was dealing with a deluge of issues inherent in unintended pregnancy while living in an untenable situation. In a way, we now share a daughter, Tessa. We both claim her, and, more importantly, Tessa claims both of us.

In the old days of closed adoption, it would have been normal for the story to have ended where it began—with a tiny, squalling baby. One of us leaving the hospital with Tessa, the other going home empty-armed. One of us a winner, one a loser.

But nothing about our situation has been "normal." Crystal and I have forged an unlikely friendship over the years as we continually cocreate our open adoption. We do this ultimately for Tessa but also for ourselves. While there is not really a word to describe our relationship—*sister* is not accurate, *friend* is insufficient—we continue to define the previously undefined. I love my daughter's birth mom. It's that simple, yet there are layers of complexity to our relationship.

How did open adoption happen so effortlessly for us? We are often asked that question. We have examined our history, and the stories of others, to find the markers of success. We find that one word captures the nature of these successful relationships: *open*. We have an open-hearted open adoption. Out of those early days of defeat and despair, we were each other's salvation. And we were wise enough to open ourselves to that.

YOU MAY ALREADY BE PRACTICED AT OPENNESS AND JUST NOT KNOW IT

The mutual-salvation aspect is an important point to make. In a well-functioning open adoption, neither party is less than the other. While both sides may be grateful to one another, neither side is beholden. There is no winner and no loser, no scale favoring one party over the other. Instead, there is mutual respect, mutual trust, and a striving for equal footing.

The word *equal* can cause some angst: Are we saying that all four of the child's parents are equally involved in raising that child? Are we expecting that a committee will convene each time a decision is made for the child? Are there an equal say and an equal do through the child's lifetime?

No, no, and no. Open adoption does not mean coparenting. It means that in the eyes of the child both sets of parents have significant value. Both sets of parents have a legitimate claim on the child and the child is able to claim both sets of parents as his own. One set is important because of biology and the other is important because of biography. To force the child to put one over the other is the reverse of the Solomon dilemma, and just as painful a choice for the child as it was for the biblical baby's "real" mother. *Equal* does not have to be a complicated concept. It simply means that you respect the role your child's other parents have in his or her life and you encourage the other parents to fill that role as only they can.

In his book *Lifegivers*, Jim Gritter describes three vital dimensions of parenting: life giving, life sustaining, and life affirming. Birth parents fill the first role, adoptive parents the second, and both types of parents share the third, along with aunts and uncles, grandparents, teachers, coaches, and others who nurture the child through his lifetime.[2] Is it possible to have too many people loving your child? Probably not. You would embrace a math teacher or a volleyball coach in doing what you cannot do for your child—why not embrace the person who can offer the life-giving or life-sustaining role that you are not able to, as well?

THIS MAY NOT BE QUITE THE STRETCH YOU THINK IT IS

You may think you don't already have a template for such a relationship, but you probably do. Do you have in-laws?

An in-law is someone who is connected to you through another person you both love. It's a person whom you didn't directly choose to have in your life but who came as part of a package deal, and in that package is someone you *do* want to have in your life. For the sake of that common person, you do your best to build a working relationship.

You may hope to simply get along and avoid conflict, but in many cases it is desirable—and possible—to actually *like* each other. When that happens, everyone wins, especially the person at the center. You're not likely to cut in-laws from your life just because you want to be the Only Important Person to your beloved.

What is most difficult for the person at the center is when either of the two he joins dislikes each other or, worse, forces him to take sides. What man wants to choose between his partner and his mother? What woman enjoys refereeing conflicts between her spouse and her father? What child wouldn't hurt when forced to choose between people who are each vitally important to him?

With in-laws, you begin with the common ground you have—the loved one at the center. You offer your respect for their position in your loved one's life, and you build from there. You might rack your brain for any common interests you might possibly share. But even if you have to really stretch to find just even one other thing, you always have that centerpiece, your loved one.

Think about in-laws or extended family members in your own life. Are you crazy about all of them? Are there any whom you merely tolerate? While mere tolerance makes having a happy relationship a bit harder, it's okay and preferable to avoiding or excluding such people.

Maybe you don't have a lot of contact or intimacy with cranky Aunt Lydia or deadbeat Cousin Bill, with controlling Uncle Lou or yakkety Grandma Mabel, but you do show up at gatherings and endure the events as best you can, and you keep the in-laws on your holiday-card list. That's what family is. After all, these foibled people are connected to your family, like it or not.

So if you ever begin to think that you just can't do this, can't share a dear one with others who have a claim on him, remember that you probably already do.

FOR ADOPTING PARENTS: THE ADOPTION PROFILE

The tool that often first brings both sets of parents together is the adoption profile, the adopting single or couple's résumé, usually a four-to-twelve-page document or an online listing. It greets expectant parents who are considering adoption, offers them some facts about you, and otherwise shows in words and photos who you are. It is placed in The Book of an adoption professional, along with profiles from other waiting couples. The profile can contain letters from each person, answers to questions posed by the agency or facilitator on the expectant parents' behalf, and photos detailing your lives.

There are many ways to make a profile visually appealing and distinct. You can begin building on your desire for openness with the tone of your profile: Compose it as an invitation to a dialogue rather than as a monologue. Invite your reader to cocreate a relationship that works for both of you, with the child at the center. Help your reader to see what choosing you will look like for not only the child but for the reader as well.

When creating our adoption profiles, my husband Roger and I followed the tips I highlighted at ProfilesThatGetPicked.com (in appendix A). We submitted it to The Book on a Wednesday. By the following Wednesday, we'd gotten The Call. We'd been picked to be parents.

CRYSTAL SAYS: I definitely wanted to choose parents for my baby. I wanted people in a strong marriage. I wanted people who didn't have any children yet. I wanted them to not be too old and not too religious. I wanted them to be fun and happy, and I wanted to like them. Not everyone wants the same things, but these were the characteristics that were important to me.

So I picked Christy and Bob. My counselor showed me a book of profiles, and I narrowed it down to choice A (Christy and Bob) and choice B (Lori and Roger). They were pretty even, but the As were a little younger than the Bs. Then two things happened.

I had Christy and Bob's profile with me, and I was so excited about it that I had to drive it over to show my family. In doing so I *lost* their profile because I had placed it on top of my car! I was so upset, freaking out—I didn't know what to do. I knew they had worked really hard on that profile, and I felt terrible! I ended up finding it later in front of my neighbor's house in the street, but the whole situation felt like a sign.

The second thing that happened was that I got a call that couple A did not want to accept the match for various reasons. I'll never know what the road not taken would have looked like, but I think that was the best thing that could have happened for all of us. That day I confirmed my B choice, Lori and Roger.

ADOPTING PARENTS COME TO THE OPEN-ADOPTION TABLE

While it's not universal, the primary reason that people seek to adopt is because of infertility—the inability to conceive, carry, and give birth to a live baby.

Some people experience biological infertility due to medical reasons like endometriosis, azoospermia, diabetes, recurrent pregnancy loss, and a host of other conditions. Others are faced with situational infertility, such as single people or gay or lesbian couples who want to become parents. Some go through fertility treatments prior to beginning the adoption process, and some go directly to adoption.

This means that many adopting parents come to the open-adoption table after an oft-repeated cycle of hope and despair, hope and despair. Their hearts have been broken; they know grief well.

Just a year after our wedding, my husband and I found out about our fertility issues right as we began a two-year stint as expatriate teachers at an international school in the Middle East. We ended up living in the same apartment building as a fertility doctor and were thus able to do a round of fertility treatment while there, which was unsuccessful. After returning home to the States, we confirmed that our odds of conceiving and birthing a child were infinitesimal. The sound of that door closing behind us was the biggest clang I never heard.

We were left with three options:

1. more fertility treatments with awful odds
2. embracing a child-free life
3. pursuing adoption

We carried in us grief from the original diagnosis of infertility, grief from our failed cycle, grief from our lost dreams, frustration at not being able to control our fate, and fear of not being able to make our dreams come true.

These emotions are the baggage we brought to the open-adoption table: grief, frustration, control issues, fear of the future.

ON THE GRIEF OF ADOPTING PARENTS

We've said before that a child deserves to come into a home as the best choice if not the first choice, into a home that is not saturated with unresolved grief. Adopting parents may have some grief work to do to make their home warm and inviting.

The process of grieving is an exercise in opening your heart and being guided by it. Perhaps you feel like your heart has been broken, sometimes more than once, and you think you can't take any more. Often it's this grief that stands between you and your goal of becoming parents. Yet forward movement comes as you process and release your grief.

On one hand, letting go of your grief might sound like the most impossible thing in the world. Maybe you'd rather have a whole army of white-gloved social workers judge every aspect of your lives than hinge your dream's fulfillment on your own healing.

On the other hand, this is within your control. For your heart has not only been broken, it has been broken *open*. Once you heal it, it is poised to bring you unimaginable happiness and fulfillment.

The question is, though, how to heal? Here are two ideas, one assisted and the other solo.

- Get a good grief therapist or attend a grief-support class. You might have one available to you through your health-care plan, or check with your local hospital for offerings.

• Write a goodbye letter to the biological child you will never have. We did this one afternoon in adoption school, and every one of us was reduced to tears—painful yet releasing tears. As you write your letter and release your dream, cry and cry and cry and cry. You are clearing the clouds so the sun can shine again.

One beneficial side effect that comes from wholly grieving our own losses is being prepared to help our adopted kids one day grieve any perceived loss they might feel. We'll have firsthand experience of coming out on the other side and will be able to abide with our children while they make their way through the shadows.

PLACING PARENTS COME TO THE OPEN-ADOPTION TABLE

Crystal, then twenty and mom to a four-year-old son, found herself pregnant by her boyfriend, Joe, who was not her son's father. Their relationship was quite volatile at the time, and Crystal felt it best for her son, her unborn baby, and herself to place the baby for adoption. She'd been in denial for the early part of her pregnancy and only arrived at an agency late in her second trimester. Once there, she was counseled around various issues—low self-esteem, healing from prior trauma, and considering her options with her baby.

Like us, Crystal had three options when finding out about her pregnancy, but her options looked very different from Roger's and mine:

1. She could choose to parent.
2. She could end the pregnancy.
3. She could place the baby for adoption.

And like us, Crystal felt out of control, not in her own driver's seat, fearful of all the unknowns and difficulties attendant in any of the paths she might choose. But from all of the options open to the three of us, adoption was the nexus that brought us to the same table—each with more than a few bags.

COMMON GROUND

Throughout this narration we've called it the *open-adoption table*, but at the time our story was unfolding neither Crystal nor my husband nor I really knew about the "open" part until the agency we both consulted told us about it.

As the final step in our home-study process, my husband and I attended three days of adoption school. At the beginning of the first day, all twelve of us in the class were told to line up along a wall and were asked to migrate to the left if we were 0 percent comfortable with open adoption and to the right if we were 100 percent comfortable. We all huddled to the left of center, around 30 percent. The adoption and pregnancy counselors on hand for our class explained that this was a common result in the classes they ran. They also asked us what we already knew about open adoption; we all admitted it wasn't very much.

A significant portion of the three days in adoption school was spent helping each of us to understand what open adoption is and what it would require from us. We were also encouraged to try on adoption from a perspective different from our own.

On the second day of class, our social workers led us in a family-sculpting exercise. Each of us twelve had a role to play—one was the expectant mother, another the expectant father. There was the adopting mom and the adopting dad. Others were parents of the expectant and adopting couples. Finally, there was the baby, which was my assignment.

Piece of cake, I thought. *Of course I'll be eager to join my forever parents, and we'll live happily ever after.*

The facilitators took us to various points in the adoption process, like finding out about the pregnancy; deciding to parent, terminate, or make an adoption plan; choosing adoptive parents; the match meeting; the birth; leaving the hospital; and the first birthday. At each point, everyone in the class was to get in a position, in relation to the others, that showed how we felt in each moment.

I really got into my part, and I was surprised at how cozy I felt being inside my mother's body. How I didn't want to leave her. How her sadness touched me. How it felt so very wrong for everything to change once I was born.

It most definitely was not a piece of cake.

With my body positioning, I didn't right away lean toward the adoptive parents. In fact, I clung to my mother and felt sadness and loss when she left me. I was surprised at these emotions—I hadn't expected them. Soon, though, I did grow to love my other parents, but it was far from seamless.[3]

I can't know what feelings I really might have had as a baby placed for adoption. But this exercise gave me a perspective I hadn't had before. And I've since come to believe that in adoption the more you can see from other points in the constellation and the more comfortable you are with your own position in it, the more compassion you can have for the others in your constellation.

CRYSTAL SAYS: I knew about open adoption, but I didn't realize the breadth and depth of it until my counselor, Amy, told me about it. I went in with expectations that I could choose my baby's parents, but Amy showed me that openness can mean so much more. "There's a range," she said, "from just knowing names to sharing photos to having phone calls and visits."

My ideas about openness were not fully formed for a while. I wanted the *possibility* of contact, but that wasn't set in stone. I just wanted the eventual parents to be people who were open to being open and to creating a relationship with me. I wanted to find people who would want the best for my baby. And I believe that included having me in the child's life.

Monika, who writes at the blog Musing Monika, placed her daughter in 2009 after giving birth four weeks early in a surprise pregnancy. Though in a stable relationship with her still-partner, he had been deployed in the military, and Monika felt unprepared to parent under such circumstances. In researching her options, Monika learned about open adoption:

> The social worker assigned to me introduced the concept as a benefit mainly to me. Only now that I've done much more research into the subject and am living it myself have I come to realize that open adoption is mainly for the children while still benefitting both the adoptive and birth parents. Strange as it may seem, I had very few hopes for my open adoption when I placed. I was so in shock about the whole thing at that point that I had no concept of having a choice in the whole matter. I didn't realize all the choices that I could have made.[4]

MEETING THE OTHERS AT YOUR OPEN-ADOPTION TABLE

One Sunday afternoon in the early spring of 2001, when Crystal was in her final month of pregnancy, her social worker facilitated a meeting with Roger and me. I was a bundle of nerves, worried about two things: One, would she like us? And two, would we like *her*? That last part might sound egotistical, but it's a legitimate concern. I was planning to be connected to this then-stranger for the rest of our lives. Wouldn't it make for an easier road if we took to each other?

My husband and I had no road map for what we wanted from our open relationship, were we to end up parenting Crystal's baby. We hadn't nailed down our open-adoption requests, such as at what point we'd exchange identifying information or how many visits we'd be comfortable with or how frequently we'd send photos. Not because we were slackers but because it seemed ridiculous to set rules for our relationship before we'd even met Crystal. After all, how well would it work if you had all the rules of your marriage set before you even met your partner? People cocreate healthy relationships *together*.

We entered the meeting room not with a plan but with an openness to being open, an eagerness to cocreate a relationship with this woman, something that would work for all of us and create the best environment possible for the baby.

Fortunately and fortuitously, Crystal entered the room with the same openness. And I was surprised later to learn that she was also worried if we would like her!

CRYSTAL SAYS: I was so nervous before the meeting and at the beginning of it. I'm not sure if I was more scared of Roger and Lori meeting *me* or of them meeting my mother, who came with me. (I was all sparkles and sunshine and my mom was, as Lori once said, like the rottweiler who had my back, the one asking the tough questions like, "You'll let the baby know about the biological family, won't you?" and "How do we know you'll keep your promises?") I didn't want them to judge me and to consider me a Loser.

At the meeting I wanted my intentions to be clear: Given what I had to work with, I wanted the best situation possible for my baby (we didn't know yet she was a girl). I felt confident in my decision but not so confident in myself. I didn't want to be judged, and I wanted them to like me. At the same time I had an inner confidence in my intentions and my plan. I knew I needed to like the people I chose as parents. I knew I needed to find the right people.

Once I saw Roger, I was done for—he's handsome! I could also tell that he was something special on the inside. And I felt so at ease with Lori right away. It was as if we'd known each other forever. My intuition flashed green lights all around, and from that meeting on I never questioned my decisions to place with them.

SELF-ASSESSMENT: IS OPENNESS A FIT FOR YOU?

If you were getting ready to attempt a triathlon or sing at open-mike night at your corner coffee shop, you might first take stock of your current skills and improve where necessary. Likewise, prior to entering into an open adoption you may wish to assess the ways in which you are ready and where you might need some stretching.

Here are some questions adopting parents should ask themselves to assess their readiness for openness:

- Can I put my child at the center of my adoption decisions?
- Am I likely to be secure in my own parenting?
- Am I able to be clear with myself about my own feelings?
- Am I able to communicate my feelings clearly, even if they are not pretty?
- If I feel jealous or angry or sad about any of our interactions, how will I deal with that?
- How well do I like the expectant parents we're matching with?
- Can I see myself in a relationship with these people years down the road?

And, equally important, here are some questions placing parents ought to ask themselves to assess their readiness for openness:

- Am I able to witness another couple raising my child and deal with the emotions that may arise?
- If I feel jealous or angry or sad about this open adoption, how will I deal with that?
- Am I able to communicate my feelings even if they aren't easy ones?
- How do I see the preadoptive parents treating others around them? Do they have a reputation for trustworthiness?
- What does my intuition say about this couple I've chosen?

Undoubtedly, once in awhile you'll have "bad" feelings, like sadness or anger or jealousy or frustration. The point of asking yourself these questions isn't to get to the place where you have only "good" or acceptable feelings. Rather, the point is to find clarity within yourself so that you are aware when you are having a negative feeling. In doing so, you are able to deal with your emotions openly rather than have them influence your thoughts and actions unconsciously. Being conscious and clear makes any human relationship healthier.

And just like you don't have to be an accomplished triathlete to participate in a triathlon, you don't have to be a master of openness to start opening your heart and life to your child's other parents. The main requirement is simply to show up at the table and open yourself to being open. With practice, you'll get better and better.

JOINT EXERCISE: SETTING UP A WAY OF RELATING

Once you've personally assessed your readiness for openness and you're both at the open-adoption table, it's time to begin your relationship together. There's an elephant in the room early in an open adoption, and you can talk about it or around it. The elephant is the fact that you are setting patterns for how to deal with each other and the complex emotions that can arise in any emotionally charged relationship. The patterns will be set either on purpose or by default, so why not make them consciously, with purpose? To help you be proactive, you might ask each other questions such as these:

- If I felt _____ (jealous, insecure, sad, angry, etc.), how would you want me to handle this with you?
- My biggest fear in this arrangement is _____. Let's talk about this.

  - Birth parent example: . . . *that you will close this adoption to me.*
  - Adopting parent example: . . . *that the child will not consider me the "real" mom.*

- Would you feel _____ (emotion) if I _____ (action)? How would you like me to handle such situations?

  - Birth parent example: . . . *Would you feel upset if I said that the baby looks just like I did when I was that age?*
  - Adopting parent example: . . . *Would you feel anxious if I invited you to the baptism?*

In having such dialogues, you may discover some of your own sore spots that still need healing. For example, let's say it would feel like a dig to you if your child's first mom were to say the child looks just like her. The first mom would likely be stating a simple observation and not intending to inflict a wound. But if you're mindful about your feelings when they arise, then when you feel that stab in your heart you are able to see it as a place that still needs healing within rather than an intentional poke from outside. Talking about it and bringing your emotions up to a conscious level allows a healing release to occur (perhaps in small increments) and prevents misunderstandings from cropping up.

So many relationship difficulties come from not knowing the other person's motives and filling that void with your own assumptions. Setting up a way to deal with each other serves the purposes of helping you to identify your own sometimes-concealed emotions, talking clearly with your counterpart about hers, and then dealing with the emotions you are both experiencing in an above-board manner, with all your cards on the table. With clarity within and between, your relationship is more likely to proceed smoothly, even through all the normal ups and downs.

You may also want to discuss who initiates contact and the preferred ways of going about it. Do you each welcome contact from the other? Should the ball be in one person's court at certain times? Do you prefer phone calls, e-mails, texts, Skype sessions, letters, or something else? Bring it up, and talk about it.[5]

GRIEVING FOR BIRTH PARENTS

While adoptive parents *come* to the open adoption table with grief (and usually leave it with joy), the birth- or expectant parents often *leave* the table with fresh grief they must process, sometimes compounded by its sister emotion, fear. Monika, of the blog *Musing Monika*, shares about her grief and fear:

> Since I was also dealing with the man I love being deployed, I attributed my missing of my daughter to be grief over missing him. It was both. My fears grew after we had our first visit six- months postplacement and after I started chatting with other birth moms. I found out how many different ways an open adoption relationship can break down, and because I'm a worrywart I had no problem magnifying those fears and applying them to my own situation. This was despite the fact that I had absolutely no factual basis for those fears. I've now recently started letting go of most of those fears after talking with my daughter's adoptive parents.[6]

Monika spoke more about her grief in an interview on an adoptive mom's blog, revealing that owning her decision and seeing her child happy brought her some peace.

> I don't think with the amount of grief that any birth mother experiences that she can be truly and completely at peace. There's a lot of guilt and shame that goes into making a decision like that, even if you know it's the best one for your child. However, I'm into taking personal responsibility for my choice. That doesn't mean I brag about it to everyone and anyone, from the tops of roofs. However, it does mean that even when I have bad grief days I don't spend my time in If Onlys and What Ifs. The decision has been made; I wouldn't go back on it even if I could, and, given similar circumstances, I'd make the same decision. Taking that responsibility for my choice and the choices I made that led me to make the choice I did has provided a huge measure of peace. It does help that I have such a great and open relationship with my daughter's parents too, and I get to see that I made a great decision—that my daughter is thriving and loved. That right there is most important of all. Even if your relationship with your child's parents is less than ideal, being able to catch little glimpses that your child is happy and loved validates the choice you made.[7]

Annie, who placed her son in 2010, explains that finding others who'd undergone the same experience and writing down her own emotions helped her deal with grief in the early months postplacement:

> I spent a couple nights hanging out with my doula and some time hanging out with another birth mom, people who had insight into what I was going through. I wish I'd had more of that—I needed to be able to talk about life and feel what I was feeling—the grief, the joy, the anger, the frustration, the worry—was normal. Soon after placement I started reading online forums and then began writing a blog. For me this was definitely a therapeutic process. I was able to talk about what I was thinking but still had some accountability to mean what I said. It really made me start looking at the way I was feeling and how I was processing my emotions. It also made me realize that I wasn't alone.[8]

Amy Hutton, of the blog *Amstel Life*, recognizes the importance of counseling, physical activity, and service.

I went to counseling at my college's counseling center. I joined groups and organizations that helped me to meet new friends. I also began swimming again (which I loved doing before my daughter was born), and it helped me to heal. Exercise was a great way for me to take my mind off the pain and concentrate on setting goals for myself. I was also able to volunteer my time by joining a student organization that advocated resources for pregnant and parenting students. We offered free babysitting and social activities for student parents on campus. In doing this, I was able to help pregnant and parenting students at my college and I was able to connect with women who I may not have otherwise been able to connect with and help. It was very therapeutic. I wish I'd started counseling immediately after my daughter was born instead of waiting until I hit rock bottom to seek help.[9]

I asked Annie, Monika, and Amy if they had advice for new birth parents. Annie thinks "every birth parent just needs to go through it; there are no shortcuts or helpful hints. No matter how bad it feels, I can almost guarantee there are other people who have felt as desperate, angry, sad, alone, lost, and guilty as you do. You're not the only person going through this, and it is okay for it to hurt."[10]

Monika's advice echoes Annie's: "Talking about it helps more than anything, like making connections on Birth Mom Buds. . . . Also, admit to people that you've placed. It doesn't have to be something you bring up in every random conversation you have. However, there's a lot of shame, even self-imposed, that can go along with a decision to place, and admitting you've done it can be a great way to accept your placement decision and start the healing process."[11]

Amy offers two tips to new birth mothers: "Get involved in activities outside your comfort zone, and make new friends. Being social can help build your self-esteem, and you'll hopefully begin to develop deep friendships with people who can help you get through the difficult times. Set goals, and do things you never thought you could. I ran a 10k after the adoption, and I felt so proud of myself for sticking to a workout plan, setting goals, and achieving those goals."[12]

When asked about the effects on grief of postplacement contact, Monika says, "A lot of birth moms believe that contact with their child and the parents after relinquishment will cause them more grief, but I've found the exact opposite to be true. Seeing my daughter thriving, happy, and, above all, loved immensely has been very helpful to me in my own healing journey. It's helped verify that I made a good choice and goes a long way to providing relief from the grief."[13]

ISSUE: PREBIRTH MATCHING

Many people hoping to adopt have visions of matching with an expectant mom sometime during her pregnancy, attending doctor's visits with her to hear the baby's heartbeat, being called to the hospital when birth is imminent, and maybe even participating in the baby's birth. In other words, experiencing those moments lost to them due to infertility, and getting in on the baby's life as early as possible. I did.

The adopting parents, though, are not the only ones with wants. Let's take a look at some of the competing needs and rights within the adoption constellation and how to balance them.

First, some assert that the baby ought to have the right to be raised by biological parents whenever possible and sensible. Second, some say that the expectant parents who are considering voluntary placement ought to have the right to make their decision whether to parent or to place freely, and without undue influence—which typically requires counseling for all parties. "But counseling that is focused on the process rather than the outcome is a rare thing," says Marcy Axness, PhD, development specialist and author of *Parenting for Peace.* "Most adoption counseling is designed to make sure the placement goes through."[14]

I asked Dr. Axness, herself an adoptee, about the risks and the rewards that can stem from prebirth matching and how she would counsel people to do it well.

> The practice of prebirth matching really begs the question, *When does an adoption begin?* Do we start arranging an adoption while the baby is still growing in the womb? Do we encourage—in either subtle or overt ways—the mom to emotionally distance herself from her child? What effects might such detachment have on the baby? One risk to the child is that the pregnant mother might feel "less than" when compared with the couple who wants to parent her baby. A huge wellspring of the baby's well-being comes from mother's own emotional and psychological state during pregnancy.

Another risk is present if the hopeful couple is coming from a place of desperation and unresolved grief. I know firsthand the feeling from the moment of birth that "everybody wants something from me." It's overwhelming for an adopted person, the feeling that I'm going to be a miracle baby, a golden child, fill all the holes from the past losses for these people who are now my parents.

Jim Gritter calls on would-be adoptive parents to shift from a "What can we get" orientation to a "What can we give" mind-set. Doing so is helpful to the pregnant mother and the baby, and *to themselves*. It's a form of enlightened self-interest to take the focus off our own lack and shift to where we are abundant and able to give. It rearranges our whole neural map, builds new brain pathways, changes the whole dynamic.

In some instances, prebirth matching could possibly help prevent the mother's emotional detachment, if done in a healthy and mindful way. If prospective adopting parents can affirm and emotionally support the pregnant mother in claiming her pregnancy, and really embracing her central importance to her baby during these months, everyone benefits. I understand, this is admittedly a tall order.

It's counterintuitive. If we encourage strong prenatal attachment, aiming for a strong bond between mother and baby, the less complicated the grieving may be for both mother and baby if the bond is severed. (We know from research that when a spouse dies, the grieving is cleaner and less complicated if that relationship was strong. The grieving process is more difficult if the relationship was shaky or ambivalent.)

A key to all of this is mindfulness and consciousness. It's the consciousness with which we do prebirth matching that makes the difference. Do we do it with a true recognition and respect for the fact that the pregnant mother is The Mother right up until the time she makes a considered choice to parent or not (which happens only after the baby is born)? Can prospective adopting parents keep their ownership needs and desperation in check? Again, that's a tall order, but it's the beginning of child-centered parenting.[15]

CRYSTAL SAYS: I see prebirth matches like fire or knives. They can be used as tools and be helpful, or they can be used as weapons to coerce and control.

Some birth-mother groups say that all matching during the pregnancy should be banned in order to keep the expectant mom from feeling as though she owes the waiting couple or is responsible for making their dreams come true. I can see how that might happen and does happen, especially if money is changing hands for expenses.

But for some women like me, a prebirth match was part of what I envisioned, what I wanted. Not for my child's parents, but for my child. Meeting Lori and Roger before the delivery enabled me to get to know them and what kind of people they are. It also let me live out the birth scenario I wanted all along, to have them there at her birth, parenting her from the first moments. Some may judge me for wanting that, but this part was important to me in getting my child set up firmly in her new family. I wanted them all to bond immediately. Which didn't mean that I wasn't part of the bonding, too—I was! There was never a moment that I didn't feel tightly connected to my baby, my daughter.

I felt empowered to have the choice of a prebirth match.

PUT YOUR TRAY TABLES UP

You've read all about your destination, checked your baggage, and boarded the plane. You know more about both adopting and about expectant parents who create an adoption around a child, and you've examined the intersecting paths of the two sets of parents. You are aware of a few of the infinite ways that openness can be launched and configured, and you're wondering just how your own may one day operate.

In the following chapter, we'll hear from people who have been-there-done-that—traveled the open adoption path—and find out from them what pitfalls and successes they encountered. Like any good traveler, you want to prevent problems but must prepared to deal with them should they arise.

4

GUIDEPOSTS FROM FAMILIES WHO HAVE TRAVELED THE PATH

When you are aware of pitfalls that can occur in open adoption and have tips on how to avoid them, you may not have to face them. And if you *do* come up against an obstacle in your open-adoption relationship, you can learn what does and doesn't work from others who have faced a similar one. A guide is in order.

Let's orient our true north as the well-being of the child. In an open-hearted open adoption, the adults who come together must be aware of their own fears and limitations as they focus on what is best, long-term, for the child. Consider this chapter your global positioning system, with markers, guidance, and signposts to help you experience the journey you desire, fashioned by those who have traveled the road before you.

Using stories from families in open adoption as well as observations by experts in the field, some potential problems are revealed. You'll read about difficulties in communication, about establishing healthy boundaries between adoptive and birth families, and about dealing with broken agreements. This chapter also offers advice on how to rebalance after experiencing a failed adoption. In addition, this chapter reveals the positive side of open adoption, distilling some common features of successful open adoptions, as told by members of the triad and adoption professionals.

Finally, upon entering an open adoption, parents may automatically become ambassadors for it, so we'll explore how to talk about it with friends and family members who think we're crazy to maintain contact.

SAFETY

Clearly, we do not suggest that anyone choose openness-with-contact in lieu of a child's or a family's safety. Openness-with-contact *assumes* safety. Abraham Maslow's theory on the hierarchy of needs supposes that if our base physiological and security needs are not met, we will not be free to pursue higher-order needs, such as relationships, self-esteem, and self-actualization.[1]

So, first things first. If there is a legitimate fear for a child's or a family's safety due to substance abuse, a violent nature, mental illness, or any other cause, staying safe takes precedence over being open-with-contact.

Be aware that children absorb their self-esteem in part from the ways in which their adoptive parents talk about the birth parents. If a child overhears a family member or family friend call his birth father a "wackadoo" or his birth mother a "crack whore," it is almost certain that those words will be deeply internalized. Sensitivity, compassion, and discretion are key.

Openness is the *spirit* in which you approach your child's biological roots as much as it is anything you *do*. You do not have to let dangerous people into your lives and your home to be in an open adoption. In such cases, you might simply honor the birth family for their part in creating your amazing child and have compassion for their difficult road. As Jim Gritter says in his book *The Spirit of Open Adoption*, "We see clearly that the spirit of open adoption is a spirit of profound honor and deep compassion. We are humbled by the gentleness and respect that is required of us."[2]

It's also important to be open to being open over time. People and circumstance can change, and if there is a safe way in the future to build a relationship with your child's birth parents, you want to be able to seize that opportunity. It's beneficial to occasionally reassess.

COMMUNICATION

Between any two given people coming together, occasional communication difficulties are bound to arise. If the relationship has a charge to it, as often happens in an open adoption, the ability to communicate assertively becomes even more crucial. But assertiveness is like Goldi-locks's just-right porridge—too much assertion becomes aggression (too hot), too little becomes passivity (too cold). And then there's the ever-dreaded passive-aggression (too mushy and lumpy at the same time), which is what people resort to when they feel completely powerless. If you dislike dealing with passive-aggressive people, do everything rea-sonable in your power to prevent their feeling powerless.

Fear can easily hinder clear communication. And what is the biggest fear confronting each set of parents in an adoption? The fear that re-sides in the dark corners of *adoptive parents'* psyches is that they will never be considered the "real" parent, that there's a convenient spare parent out there ready to take over at any time. The fear that most often clouds *birth-parent* communication is that the adoptive parents will close the adoption, the birth parents powerless to stop it. These fears can make trusting one another in this delicate relationship a challenge and can make clarity within oneself and between parties difficult.

The fear of not being the "real" parent is a fascinating one, because when we demand to be considered the "real" parent, often what we're manifesting is not our need for *others* to find us legitimate but, way deep down in our innermost selves, our *own* fear that we are not the legitimate parent.

One mom asked for communication help in an adoption forum on a thread she called "Why Can't I Just Say *No* When the [Birth Mother] Does Stuff That Is Not Okay!" Jessica C. explains her problem:

> It is the second time [the birth mother] has taken out our son from his car seat while the car is moving. What in the world causes me to choke up and not scream the words that are racing through my mind! *Who in the world takes a baby out of a car seat when the car is moving!* I am struggling to fight this speechlessness that overcomes me! Part of it is that we are still trying to build a trusting relationship with her and we are a work in progress. Part of it is that she is doing something I just can't believe anyone would do and I seem to go into some idiotic state of shock.
>
> In a pathetic and mouse-like voice, I have stated, "He needs to be back in his seat," but she ignores me, because who would take that lack of authority seriously?
>
> It's just something about her being his [birth mother]. The re-spect that I work so hard to uphold for her, the gratitude that I feel

for the gift she has given us, everything she has done in choosing us to raise our son.

I am so mad at myself. I am not a passive person, I am not a doormat, but with her, and her relationship to our son, I just become this other person. When she arrives, I move to the sidelines to give her the time with our son. I know that the problem lies with the fact that she is his [birth mother] and somewhere in that, I'm overcompensating.[3]

While Jessica is disturbed by the actions of the birth mom, she also is wise to know that the problem and the solution are hers, as she asks how to better handle her acquiescence. The main thing she needs to do? Fully move into her role as the mom of her son. From there, right words and right actions will flow. Remember how we learned that open-adoption relationships are much like in-law relationships? If Jessica imagined herself in the same situation but replaced the birth mother with a sister-in-law, she would have no trouble finding her voice, asserting herself, fully occupying the role of Mama Bear. With words she might say, "Our car doesn't move unless everyone is buckled in." With actions she might pull over and calmly say, "I'm sorry, our family's policy is to always be buckled in. I'll resume driving when he's secure again. Please ask first in the future before you take him out so I can pull over safely ahead of time. This way we're obeying the law and keeping our son safe."

Sometimes simply asking, "How would I handle this if it were Cousin Billy or Aunt Mary?" will help make communication flow more easily in an open-adoption relationship.

Annie, a birth mom we heard from in chapter 3, says that she sometimes has difficulty communicating her feelings to her son's dads because of assumptions she makes about their possible reaction.

There were times I was so scared of how they *might* react that I allowed my fear to talk me out of doing or saying something I wanted to. I get so afraid of what might play out instead of just doing what my gut tells me. Pushing too hard could fracture our relationship. I want to hope that our relationship isn't so fragile, that it could withstand any miscommunication. But until I'm more sure of that, the stakes of possibly losing this level of contact with my son is too much to risk. So instead I tend to stay quiet more often than not, to be cautious of how much I push them.

I think they are fine having me in their life because I pose no threat; I don't know at what point I might start posing a threat and they might be uncomfortable with me. And that's why I don't push, because I just don't feel like I know the boundaries.[4]

Clear communication is based on trust, and it sounds like Annie and her son's parents have not yet reached a trusting level of intimacy. But they could. Either on their own or perhaps with a counselor—a social worker who assisted with their adoption, if available—the three of them could do the exercise we learned in chapter 3, "Setting Up a Way of Relating." This would give Annie a safe place to explain her fears, check her assumptions and strengthen her voice, and also deal with any fears and assumptions that her son's parents may be carrying about her. The relationship would then come more into balance with the "equal footing" we seek in a successful open adoption. Annie would no longer feel like a supplicant.

In *Hospitious Adoption*, Jim Gritter uses hospitality as the model for an adoption relationship. The first parents are the first hosts for the baby—especially the first mother. At placement, the adoptive parents then become hosts for the baby, who grows to become a toddler, a teen, and finally an adult. The adoptive parents are also the hosts of the birth parents during this time, making them feel welcome in their home and in their lives. Lastly, the adult adoptee will ultimately become the host of both sets of parents. Gritter speaks of the first shift in hosting:

> The shift of permanent authority between the families is a critical juncture that tests their capacity to provide and receive hospitality. If the transition is not handled well, birth parents are at risk to go though the adoption experience as perpetual supplicants. This is a startling prospect. One might suppose that adoptive parents would offer reciprocal hospitality as a matter of course once they have been officially installed as the legal parents. After all, they are no longer strangers to each other. What is more, the original hosts have blessed them in an incomparable manner. Sadly, though, these factors do not always translate into reciprocal hospitality. It turns out that the birth families still seem scary to the newly installed parents, possibly scarier than ever now that they have something wonderful—a child—to lose.[5]

Adoptive parents, it is in your best interest to enable your child's birth parents to feel as if they can be clear and honest with you rather than fearful of you. You would not want any other extended family member to be fearful of what you might do if he or she revealed honest thoughts to you. You would not want any important guests in your lives to feel unwelcome in your home. When your child becomes the host of your adoption relationships, when he begins to model to you what you have modeled for him, you will want to have shown kindness, trust, connection, and compassion.

BOUNDARIES

It's quite a feat to establish healthy boundaries. On one hand, you want boundaries protective enough to keep "bad" things out. But you also want them open enough to let "good" things in. It may be helpful to examine exactly how you define the bad and the good before attempting to put boundaries in place for your open adoption.

Once relinquishment and finalization happen, the adoptive family is in charge of the relationship. So for this discussion we'll focus on the adoptive family setting boundaries, which the birth family usually has very little influence over. Being at the mercy of the adoptive family is a lament we often hear from birth parents.

For Laura and Rick, who lived in the same town as their son's birth parents, Jania and Austin, the bad things they wanted to keep out consisted of unexpected visits, too many phone calls or e-mails, confusion with titles, and unvetted people the birth parents might bring into their lives. The good was comprised of tending a natural relationship between their son and his birth parents, having ongoing access for medical, behavioral, and emotional purposes, and enjoying a relationship with the two people who helped them build their family.

So Laura and Rick did what they would have done in any other close relationship with in-laws or extended family members. They simply told their son's birth parents to please make sure to prearrange any visit. They said that they welcomed calls and e-mails to their son and would let the birth parents know and figure out how to best proceed if they saw signs that it was too much for their son or the family. Laura asked, at least for the time being, that she be known as the mom and Jania as the birth mom; likewise with the dads' titles. Finally, Laura and Rick would want to get to know any person Jania or Austin brought around—a friend, boyfriend, girlfriend, or other relative—before inviting them into their lives. Putting forth these few requests, Laura and Rick hoped to have a healthy and robust relationship with Jania and Austin.

Notice what terminology Laura and Rick did not use. They did not say, "We are willing to send pictures each month." They did not say, "We consent to four visits a year." Whenever adoptive parents use words such as *willing to* and *consent to*, they are likely missing the spirit of openness and are instead operating from a place of fear, possibly setting up an adversarial relationship. As Jim Gritter says in *Lifegivers*, "Open adoption is less a set of behaviors than it is an emotional and spiritual connection."[6] You do not "consent to" having a relationship with someone with whom you feel an emotional and spiritual connection.

If you find yourself thinking in terms of what you will "grant" birth parents, what you will "give up" to them, then it's possible that, instead of seeing your relationship as mutually beneficial and having a valid place in your child's life, you view them as an imposition. At times like this, it would be helpful to ascertain what fears lurk behind those thoughts. Of course, if you have real fears for your family's safety, then your relationship may end up being somewhat adversarial. But if your fears are your personal demons—like a fear of not being the "real" parent—then the work to be done is on yourself.

Jania and Austin appreciated knowing what Laura and Rick wanted from them and were happy to comply with what they perceived to be reasonable requests. Over the years the son at the center of their relationship has reaped from their openness all of the "good" without suffering any of the "bad."

Yeah, but.

What about the birth mother who repeatedly shows up unannounced? What about the birth father who buys our daughter Mountain Dew even though we don't allow soda? What about the birth grandmother who calls herself Grammy even though we've asked her not to? What about the birth grandfather who gave our son a toy gun against our wishes?

Again, we return to modeling an open adoption relationship on in-law and extended-family relationships. Considering the questions the following way takes the "adoption charge" out of the picture:

- What would you do if your mother-in-law repeatedly showed up unannounced?
- How would you handle it if Aunt Susie gave your daughter a Mountain Dew?
- What would you do if your father-in-law asked you to call him Dad even though you already have a dad?
- How would you handle it if for your son's fifth birthday Uncle Billy gave him a toy gun, despite your family's policy?

There are dozens of ways you could handle each boundary issue. With each case, you must decide whether you will accommodate the other person's behavior and be the one to make an adjustment or whether it's worth standing firm and inviting accommodation from the other. It's also important to consider whether or not you're dealing with a one-time annoyance or a long-term problem.

The issue of the unannounced visitor is a long-term one. If it truly made my life more difficult for my family, it would be worth standing firm: "Joyce, I know you love to see your grandchildren, and they love to see you, too, but when you arrive without letting us know you run the risk of not getting our attention—you know how busy things get with all the kids' activities. Also, I respect you and would like the chance to clean up before you come. So, please, give us some notice, and get a green light first. Would you do that for us?"

If Aunt Susie gave my daughter a Mountain Dew at a special occasion, I wouldn't sweat it. If the dietary rule breaking was a pattern, though, and Aunt Susie was indulging Tessa often, I would reiterate my request that she "please stick with water or juice. The sugar and artificial colors in sodas make bedtime hard for all of us, and I know you don't want to make things hard for Tessa, right? We are teaching her to make good decisions for herself, and we need for you to be part of this teaching. Will you do that for us, for Tessa?"

As for the moniker, I would be thrilled to call my husband's parents Mom and Dad. Of course they wouldn't replace my own mom and dad. Having a spare set of parental figures who love me would enhance my life, not detract from it. I'd have more people who claim me and whom I claim. This one is an easy one for me to accommodate.

I admit that if we had an antigun stance and Uncle Billy knew about it I'd be ticked off if he still gave my son a toy gun. It would feel disrespectful, and, should I choose to take the gun away or replace it with another gift, it would put me in the position of being the Bad Guy with my son. So, then, how to best deal with each issue: the toy itself and my feelings of being disrespected? Privately, I could say to Uncle Billy, "You just broke one of our very few rules for gift giving, and, more importantly, you broke our trust. We don't want to have to screen your gifts, but unless you show us that you will respect our boundaries about this, that's what will have to happen."

On the other hand, maybe it wasn't worth engaging in combat on this issue. My son, Reed, was turning sticks, bottles, and even carpet lint into "shooters" before he was able to walk. Maybe the antigun stance was going to prove to be a losing battle and we'd be better off with a strategy other than zero-tolerance. If so, the issue about disrespect for our boundaries would remain. I might gently point out, "Billy, do you see what just happened? We had asked you not to bring guns into our home, and then you brought a gun into our home. How do you think that makes us feel? And what do you think that makes us want to do about you and gift giving?" The goal is to get Billy to see the situation from my perspective, which is always helpful in communicating and setting boundaries.

BROKEN AGREEMENTS

Sometimes we think an open adoption is going to look one way but ends up looking another. In this section we're addressing not only a formalized, written agreement (which we'll discuss later in this chapter) but also an informal understanding.

Rarely do parties get upset about an adoption becoming more open. Rather, what causes grief is when one side or another begins to close down. Danielle Pennell, adoptive mom and community moderator at the Adoptive Families Circle forums, tells how she helps her son deal with an adoption that closed unexpectedly.

I overheard my nine-year-old son Keith say to his friend, "Texas? I was born in Texas! My birth parents still live there. But," he said, "they don't call or write to me. I'm not sure why."

His friend's face looked shocked as he loudly responded, "Well, that's just rude!"

"Yeah," continued Keith, "but my mom writes them letters and sends them pictures of me. She tells them how I'm doing. But I just want to know if they are okay. I really hope they'll listen to my mom and start to write me."

His friend nodded his head as if this all made sense to him. Then he added, "That's cool what your mom is doing." "Yeah, it is cool," agreed Keith.

I was proud of him for talking about his adoption proudly and casually. Every year I send a letter and photos to our agency, and then they attempt to contact the birthparents to let them know that the update is available. This is so different from the very open relationship we had before Keith's birth until the time he was six months old or so. At that point, the weekly phone calls and letters mailed directly to each other began going unanswered. There was one short phone call on Keith's first birthday, which reaffirmed to me that they were still thinking of him. But since then, our once open relationship has become one-sided.

Has it been hard for me to write annual updates not knowing if Keith's birth parents appreciate my efforts to inform them about our amazing son, or even if they receive them? Has it been difficult to write them with questions, which Keith wants answers to, knowing that they'll likely go unanswered? Absolutely. I always find it emotionally draining to write these letters.

To make it easier for me to write these annual updates, I began mentally approaching them as a Journal of Keith. I keep a copy of each letter in a safe place and will eventually bind them together. They will be an accurate portrayal of Keith's childhood.

Hearing Keith and his friend agree that I was "cool" for writing letters and sending pictures made my heart swell. It confirmed for me that he truly understood what I was doing and why I was doing it. I know that he desires to hear from his birth parents and that he recognizes that I'm trying to make that happen by writing the letters. Even if I'm not successful, when he's older he'll know I never gave up, that I always had faith that I was establishing a connection.

I share this story to inspire you to keep your hopes up if you aren't hearing from your child's birth parents. Keep writing letters.

Keep sending pictures. Let your child know that you recognize how important this relationship is and that you are doing all you can to make it work. Your child will notice and appreciate your hard work. What better way to show respect to your child's birth parents and appreciation for your child's adoption than making every effort possible?[7]

Danielle was wise in recognizing that she could control only her own actions, not those of her son's birth parents. She had determined at the beginning of their open-adoption relationship that doing her part to stay in touch was the right thing to do, and nothing, not even nonreciprocation, stopped her from doing what she deemed best for her son.

LisaAnne is a first mother in the Midwest who was parenting three sons as a divorced mom when she became pregnant with a daughter. She and her boyfriend matched with a couple through a mutual friend, and through the pregnancy LisaAnne and the hopeful parents set patterns for how LisaAnne hoped their open adoption would look.

During my pregnancy I told them we would just let it go and see how our open adoption developed. I never wanted to intrude on their life with this child. I wanted them to feel like they were the parents. I expected that we would continue our friendship and interaction that we had developed during the pregnancy. We never talked about visits or had a formal plan. We talked about it being child-driven, focused on the daughter we all loved—Brit.

While I was pregnant, we talked all the time—on the phone, in person, and via e-mail. She went to every single doctor's appointment with me. I included her on everything. I shared when Brit started to kick, when she was giving me fits at night, and we always talked about the silly hiccups she constantly had. We went to dinner a couple of times; we were great friends.

We didn't make a plan because, honestly, I never ever dreamed I would need one. I had made a new friend. The woman who would be Brit's mom seemed like she was one of my sisters. We got along great. There was absolutely nothing that made me think that would ever change.

During the hospital stay after Brit was born, we had the new parents stay at the hospital with us. Their family came in and out of my hospital room all the time. We even all had a pizza party—me, in all of my postpartum glory, hosting a family get-together with Brit's parents' families. It felt like we were all in this together. I was happy. This is exactly how I envisioned our relationship—one big extended family all loving one child.

But after leaving the hospital, things changed. After more than two months of silence, I got up the courage to ask Brit's mom by e-mail if I could meet her for lunch with Brit before she had to go back to work. That is when she e-mailed back and said she didn't mean to be disrespectful but they weren't comfortable with that yet.

That was one of the very worst days of my life.

After several more months of silence, I sent an e-mail to Brit's dad and asked what I had done that had kept Brit's mom from e-mailing me. He called me the next morning, and it was a real eye-opener. I found out that Brit's mom was dealing with infertility grief, a struggle with feeling like she wasn't completely bonding with Brit as her mom. Also, pictures I was sending monthly of my kids and me made her realize Brit looks like me, and it upset her.

It was then that I tried to stop focusing on what I didn't have and be my best self, meaning continue doing what I thought was right. We did eventually have a two-hour visit, shortly after Brit's first birthday. That was a year ago. I continue to send cards and care packages on holidays and special days. I don't want to stop doing those things, because I consider them friends. They may not share the same sentiments, but I have had to come to terms with that. I decided that I wasn't going to let that change how I feel and acted toward them.

We live ten minutes away but are continents away in our desires for our open-adoption relationship. I own my part by not being clear from the beginning about what I wanted our postadoption relation-ship to look like. I had no idea. And they had no idea how they would feel postadoption either. We had no way to know what was about to hit all of us. If only we had.[8]

Like Danielle, LisaAnne decided to continue doing her part in hold-ing up an informal agreement—sending letters once a month about her and her boys. She does what is within her power to do, still respecting the boundaries the adoptive parents have set. She works on releasing the rest, feeling her pain but not allowing it to paralyze her.

REBALANCING AFTER A FAILED ADOPTION

Once in awhile, a placing parent decides, after all, not to place. The emotions around this look different depending on which part of the constellation you inhabit. If you are the child, you will not split your biology and your biography. If you are the biological parent, you will enjoy all the responsibilities, tribulations, and joys that come with raising a child. And if you are the one who was hoping to be this child's parent, your heart is shattered. You have likely given all you have, opened your heart freely to the baby and his parents, and now you must somehow go through it all again. But how?

Meg experienced a failed match when trying to adopt her second child.

I was aware that expectant mothers had to make up their minds all over again once they met and held their baby, but I didn't believe it could happen to us. We had such a good relationship with the expectant parents—the mom and I texted almost every day, I'd attended multiple ultrasounds, and everything seemed to be going so well.

But after the baby was born the birth parents took her home. The father said they just needed some time with her—they'd sign the papers three days later. Those days of limbo were some of the hardest in my life. I felt so very helpless, and the uncertainty was so very difficult. The mom sent me a text message apologizing for the stress this was causing us and that she didn't want us to provide financial assistance anymore since they were unsure that they would place. I decided to *act as if* she made the decision to parent, just to get myself out of limbo. This was absolutely the best thing I could have done for myself, for then I was free to begin the grieving process. I cried. A lot. I got angry at the situation, throwing the couch pillows hard onto the floor again and again. I prayed, talked, and cried some more.

I had waited to share the baby's name and birth details with friends and extended family, as I'd wanted to announce when we brought her home. The next day I shared a "birth announcement" with the baby's name and birth details, adding that I thought it was doubtful we'd be bringing her home. These actions allowed me to begin to grieve and heal. We received confirmation two days later that they had decided to parent, and I was able to take this news more in stride because I'd already been *acting as if*.

I found an article that suggested I attend an infant-loss support group. This struck me as odd, as I didn't have a baby die and I wasn't sure I'd fit in. But I took a risk and attended a meeting sponsored by SHARE (www.nationalshare.org). While our situations were very different, I could immediately relate to the feelings of grief and loss that other attendees were experiencing. We all had issues with friends and family not knowing what to say so not saying anything. After my first meeting a woman assured me "you belong here; we both went home from the hospital with empty arms." I've also started seeing a therapist every other week, which gives me an opportunity to share and get feedback one-on-one.

We have made the decision to try to adopt again, and we are currently on the list waiting to be matched. There was some fear in the decision to open ourselves up to such a potentially difficult experience again. What is helping me during this time is a concept Lori introduced me to while we were in limbo. It's called *the in-between space*.[9]

Meg is talking about a post I wrote on my blog after reflecting on my own time in limbo, during which I feared my son had a brain tumor.[10] I wrote to Meg as she waited for the parents to decide on adoption—or not: *When you feel yourself going into fear, breathe. Come to the present moment where all is well. Pain comes from living in the past, and anxiety comes from living in the future. One you can't change, and the other doesn't even exist, so you might as well stay present. You are going to be living in the Space Between, so get comfy.*

Meg says this notion helped her become aware of and dismiss her mind chatter and focus on the present moment. "This advice, the group support, and the individual therapy have given me the courage to try to adopt once again."[11]

Within a year, Meg and her husband finalized the adoption of their son, their second child.

COMMON FEATURES OF AN EFFECTIVE OPEN ADOPTION

It served Meg well that she was able to open herself up again, for openness was what helped her be chosen by her son's birth parents, and openness helped her cocreate the scenario she wanted for her family.

So, then, what are the ingredients that tend to produce an effective—even successful—open adoption? Here are a few that are integral.

1. *The obvious—being open.* A successful open adoption begins with the simple openness to being open. Open to the relationship, open to the people who are important to your child, open to possibilities. Open to giving and receiving. Open to information. Dawn Davenport, executive director of the nonprofit Creating a Family, puts it this way: "The key to success with open adoption is more of an attitude rather than specific list of do's and don'ts. *Openness* means an openness of spirit—an openness of heart—by both the first family and adoptive family. The willingness to risk possible misunderstandings, the working through issues, the having another set of family to accommodate in your life, all for the good of the child you both love."[12]

   There is a vulnerability to being open, so we begin an open adoption the way we begin any potentially intimate relationship—with the strength to be vulnerable. Quite the oxymoron.

2. *Having clarity, honesty, and trust.* These are three facets of the same trait—truth. The first is *understanding* what is true for you, the second is *offering* truth to another, and the third is expecting to *receive* truth. The day Crystal was to leave the hospital without Tessa, she took the time to be clear about her own feelings, which enabled her to be honest with me about them, which allowed me to trust in the process just a little more easily. The clear channels established that day have been in place for more than twelve years and will endure throughout our lifetimes.

3. *Letting go of fear.* Tara, a new adoptive mom, says "an important trait is to let go of fear of the unknown. It's a different way to build a family, and we are pioneers. No one in our immediate families has adopted before."[13]

   Monika Zimmerman echoes this sentiment, but from the birthparent side, saying what's important is "not being afraid of what the future might or might not bring. Realizing that each open adoption relationship is different and that just because ours is different than any other open-adoption relationship that I know about doesn't mean that it's doomed for failure."[14]

4. *Being child centered.* Crystal says, "The most important person in the relationship is the child. It was less about me or Lori and Roger than it was about Tessa. With her presence so large in the center, there was little room for the rest of us to bring our egos. We've been pretty good about leaving them outside the relationship."[15]

5. *Honoring each others' roles.* Monika says that "both Nick [the birth father] and I respect our daughter's parents as her parents. This means that we make a conscious effort to not overstep boundaries."[16] Likewise, adoptive parents in effective open adoptions honor the role that birth parents play in their children's lives— their very existence. We do this by not asking the child to rank or choose biography over biology, or vice versa.

6. *Persevering.* "We were counseled that you don't ever stop asking, offering, and giving," says Bobbie Havens of JourneytoFamily .net. "At some point [the birth parents] have to let you in, especially when you are not asking for anything but their time and a photo."[17]

7. *Being flexible.* Bobbie also advises that "you have to be willing to bend, twist, and turn, just like a plant grows toward the light. The more you can demonstrate and role model flexibility for your child, the better they will be able to do it too."[18]

   Adoptive mom Julie Mudd adds to this notion: "It's best to have flexibility in dealing with time schedules. We try to arrange our visits to the birth families so they can include their extended family members and enjoy ample time with our child."[19]

SO NOW YOU ARE AN AMBASSADOR

People around you may think it "weird" that the two sets of parents know each other, see each other, respect each other, even love each other. In the days of closed adoption, the birth family was to disappear, never to be seen, heard from, or wondered about again. Both families were to proceed as if there were not an easily apparent seam in the fabric of their lives.

In the open era, however, we know the seam is there—for both families. The birth parents have experienced a "childectomy." But instead of a hidden, festering sore, the healing happens in the open. The adoptive parents have grafted a family member onto their tree, one related by love rather than biology, much like a marriage. We are not ashamed that there is a seam. Why would we be?

Others may still rather avert their eyes or speak from the days of secrecy and shame, and here is where we become teachers, ambassadors. Here is where we vanquish the shame and fear that used to go along with adoption.

Most people don't mean to be intrusive or rude. Most questions you receive will come from curiosity and ignorance. The cure for ignorance is education, so one of your options in such encounters is to educate. You may also, at times, choose to disengage, to use humor (or even slight sarcasm), to invoke privacy (which is different from secrecy, because it carries no shame), or to ask a question back. Factors in your decision include the relationship (or lack thereof) you have with the asker, whether or not your child is within earshot, the demeanor of the asker, and your intuition as to how to best respond. Here are some examples.

- *Who are her real parents?* Do you mean her birth parents? We are both real—let me pinch you to show I'm not fake! Her birth parents live in Cincinnati. We see them twice a year and Skype regularly.

- *Aren't you afraid she'll come to take him away?* Why would she do that? She knows this would hurt him, and, clearly, she puts her love for him above everything else.

- *Why did she give her child away?* Do you mean why did she place? Though she loves her dearly, she had some private reasons that I'm not at liberty to disclose. Rest assured, though, she was very mature and loving about the whole thing. We adore her; she's part of our family.

- *Are they really brother and sister?* You've seen them bicker, haven't you? If you're asking if they have the same birth parents, no, they don't. But they are brother and sister.

- *Where did you get them?* We adopted them at birth, so at the hospital like lots of people. *Or,* We adopted them through foster care. *Or,* In Wichita—where did you get yours?

- *Couldn't get pregnant, huh?* Ummm . . . I'm wondering why my reproductive health is your business. Why would you ask about that?

- *How much did she cost?* We paid for services, much as you did with your C-section. Do you know how much your insurance company paid the doctors and the hospital for that? Oh, I probably shouldn't ask because that's kind of a private thing. *Or,* You know we didn't buy a baby, right? Baby selling and buying are illegal.

- *Don't you think she'll run away someday to her real parents?* There's a chance she'll want to run away—many kids do. It's healthy when a child has another responsible adult to turn to in times of angst. I had my Aunt Denise who counseled me to work things out with my parents—who did you have when you wanted to run away? Oh, and let me pinch you to show you I'm real.

The more comfortable you are with your story, the more easily you'll be able to talk about it and form healthy boundaries around talking about it. This is an important point and bears repeating: *The more comfortable you are with your story, the more easily you'll be able to talk about it and form healthy boundaries around talking about it.*

(Too bad, though. Our ambassadorships do not come with diplomatic immunity, and we must still feed parking meters.)

ISSUE: OPEN-ADOPTION AGREEMENTS

An open-adoption agreement can be as simple as the two families living by the statement *We all agree we will put the child at the center of our open-adoption decisions*, or it can be as involved as a formalized written agreement (often called a *post-adoption contact agreement*, or PACA).[20] Some states even allow for legal enforcement of written agreements, with rules for who may enter into such an agreement, what can be agreed upon, and what shall happen if the agreement is broken. ChildWelfare.gov says, at the time of writing, that "approximately twenty-six states and the District of Columbia currently have statutes that allow written and enforceable contact agreements."[21]

So, what are the benefits to formalizing an open-adoption agreement, either the legally enforceable kind or the "gentlemen's agreement" kind?

A formal agreement requires that each party be clear as to what he or she wants from the arrangement and will give to the arrangement, which means that expectations are clarified and expressed. How many visits and how often and where? Photos and phone calls? Birthdays and milestones? Whatever is discussed ahead of time can be thought through individually and worked out collaboratively.

In a state with enforcement, a court-approved contract can also be court-enforced. In such cases there are teeth in the agreement. This protects primarily birth parents, as they would have recourse if they felt that the adoptive parents promised one thing but delivered another.

Such an agreement serves as a reminder of the commitment each parent makes to keep the child at the center of the open-adoption relationship.

Likewise, there are some possible drawbacks to having an open-adoption agreement. Drawing up a legally enforceable document could assume an adversarial relationship between the adoptive and birth families. Furthermore, codifying emphasizes the letter of the relationship rather than spirit of the relationship. And consequences and enforcement remain problematic. For example, if a first father closes the adoption, what, realistically, would the adoptive parents do—drag him into court and force him to visit the child on schedule? And on the flip side, first mothers have told me that even if the adoptive parents did begin to close the adoption, the first parents would never risk ruining an already precarious relationship by taking adoptive parents to court, or by even threatening to do so. "And besides," one birth mom said, "where would I get the money to do that?"

The Golden Rule must infuse the spirit of any open-adoption agreement, formal or informal. It's beautiful in its simplicity: treat the other person the same way you would like to be treated were your positions reversed. This requires that we act with awareness and compassion and see from the viewpoint of another. It is a skill that helps us be better parents and better people, and we want our children to learn from us how to do it.

WE'RE ON OUR WAY

We've talked about the lay of the land, how to best avoid swamps, volcanoes, and quicksand, and what to do if you get caught in any. We know that clarity within each person and honesty between persons can result in a smoother journey. We've grown comfortable with the idea of being ambassadors for this curious relationship we've entered into, and now, as we enter part 2 we're going to explore the view from a third vantage point—that of the adoptee, an open-adoption relationship's raison d'être.

Part II

Orienting on the Child: Open Adoption's True North

Now that you know many of the reasons *why* to create an open adoption, it's time to get to the nitty-gritty of *how*.

In part 2 we shift the focus from the grownups in the constellation to the baby who becomes a toddler, then a gap-toothed kid, a tween, a teen, and finally a young adult—and who has, along the way, thoughts and opinions and desires about adoption all her own. Like many personality facets, some of these thoughts and opinions will result from how you handle things with her, and some of them are innate to her.

How do you deal with your son's adoption grief? How do you respond the first time your daughter says, "You're not my real mom"? How do you make it okay when differing levels of openness exist between your children and their respective birth parents? How do you help your son come to terms with his fantasy life, the one he's not living?

In the coming chapters we'll see openness from the adoptee's perspective (chapter 5). We'll take a peek into some challenging and intimate adoption-parenting moments, discovering what has worked well for children and parents alike (chapter 6). We'll have a reality check, figuring out what to do when things get rough (chapter 7). We'll see how to apply openness to international and foster adoption as well as donor egg, sperm, and embryo situations (chapter 8). And we'll have a special chapter to support first parents (chapter 9), finally sending you off on your open-adoption journey (chapter 10).

But before we dive in, let's refresh our memory: *Adoption creates a split in a person between his biology and his biography. Openness in adoption is an effective way to heal that split.*

5

OPENNESS AND THE ADOPTEE

The overarching theme in an open-hearted open adoption is to help the child integrate the split that can come from having two sets of parents.[1] The less emotional distance a son (or daughter) perceives between the two sets, the less divided his loyalties will be and the more integrated his psyche can be.

Does this mean the two sets of parents move in next door to each other? Take vacations together? Coparent? Not at all (unless you want it to). This emotional distance refers not to geographic space but to emotional space, a gap your child may perceive when talking to one of you about the other and to any angst that churns while trying to hold you all in his heart.

I intuitively knew when Roger and I began formulating our open adoption that in loving our children's birth parents we were giving our kids a precious gift, which in turn helps them fully love themselves. In addition, our aim is for Tessa and Reed to never feel as if they need to choose or to divide their loyalties between their birth parents and my husband and me.

I received validation that I was achieving my goal on the morning of my son's ninth birthday. "You're my favorite-favorite son!" I hugged him good morning. In response, he hugged me back and said, "You're my fave—err . . . you're one of my favorite mommies!"

There are two ways I could have interpreted his proclamation: either that I am in competition with his birth mom and I'm not out-and-out winning it, or that my son's heart is so big that he can hold us both in it.

The former notion would cause me pain and jealousy; the latter would fill me with joy and pride. Which one do you think I chose?

It can be a lot of work to remove emotional distance between you and your child's other parents. And this isn't work you do on someone else (always we want to change the other person!) but work you do on yourself.

EMBRACING OPEN ADOPTION

A reader of my blog, a mother via donor eggs, once asked what made it possible for me to invite my children's other parents into our lives with open arms. Why did I embrace open adoption so fully? And how?

The questions made me think. Early on, I had made the conscious decision to not only accept but *love* our story, warts and all. Every spiritual lesson I'd learned previously was preparing me to embrace open adoption.

A wise man once told me that being grown-up means seeing things the way they are instead of how you wish they were. Once I became a parent, I had a conscious choice to make each day, each moment: I could lament the fact that I did not give birth to my children and that my DNA and my husband's did not swim in their veins, or I could be ecstatic that my children were who they were. In other words, I could see my life in a way that made me sad and frustrated, or I could see my life in a way that made me fulfilled and happy. It is only when I'm *not* conscious that I choose the former; but when I'm making the choice with full awareness, it's sensible and easy to choose the latter.

This does not mean that I wear rose-colored glasses and never let myself think about what isn't. Instead, adoption, for both me and for my children, is about becoming whole, about the freedom to wonder, explore, question, and ultimately accept. I *do* examine the feelings I have when I notice Tessa has a set of toes that look nothing like mine, or when Reed demonstrates a talent that clearly didn't come from me. I *do* consider what parenting them might be like if we shared common ancestry. Would I understand her learning styles better? His coping mechanisms?

But I don't get stuck in these thoughts. I think them, feel them, release them. If the aphorism commonly attributed to Carl Jung is true, *that which we resist persists*, then we need to be able to think a scary thought or feel a scary emotion in order to release that same fear. Otherwise the scary thought or emotion has and builds power; power over us.

We neutralize the scariness when we are able to allow the thoughts to *move through* us and not *get stuck in* us. And what's more? We show our kids that "icky" thoughts and feelings don't have to be scary. In fact, they can be illuminating and, eventually, liberating.

Every spiritual avenue I've steeped myself in teaches that at each moment I can live from love or from fear. Love is rooted in abundance and is unlimited, originating from our true, divine nature. Fear comes from separation and from our false self, our ego. Our small, scared, limited ego.

In some ways, "Just embrace" is so much easier than "Just adopt." After all, there is no paperwork, no white-gloved social worker, no proving myself to an external authority, no power outside me deciding the outcome.

And for that same reason, "Just embrace" is so much more difficult than "Just adopt." For only I can do it. No one will tell me if I am doing it well. It's all me, all the time, just trying to stay aware of my motives and fears and consciously choosing love and embracing wholeness at every turn.

I want to show my children it can be done. I bet you do, too.

Let's look at some situations in which an adopted child is faced with her adoptedness.

QUESTIONS FROM PEERS

We begin with the child's perspective on having so many parents, both in number and in type. Perhaps the most common myth about open adoption is that the child will be confused with so many parents in the picture. Your child may be asked by other children, or even by adults, questions such as *What about your real parents? Why didn't your real mom want you? Doesn't being adopted make you different, special? Do you get extra Christmas presents since you have so many parents? When you grow up will you go live with your real mom and dad?*

Parents may not be able to prevent these questions and comments, but they can prepare their daughter to deal with them—not only with words but also with a deep understanding of her own worth and value, an integration of all her parts. Here is where you lay a firm foundation so that your child is firmly rooted in her open adoption and can withstand gentle ignorance as well as blowing windbags. In short, you're going to show and teach your child what you learned in chapter 4 about handling inquiring minds that want to know.

Experts suggest several strategies to deal with sensitive questions. The W.I.S.E. Up! program was created by the Center for Adoption Support and Education and teaches the child to assess the person asking (friend or bully?), the situation (private or in front of a group?), and how the question makes them feel (shy, happy, confused, embarrassed?). Then from this assessment the child can choose a response from the following options:

- **W**alk away.
- Say "**I**t's private."
- **S**hare something about your adoption story.
- **E**ducate with general information. [2]

And beyond the suggestions from W.I.S.E. Up!, your child has even more options:

- *Question.* "Why are you asking?"
- Deflecting or changing the subject
- Using humor

Ways to handle the question *Why didn't your real mom want you?* might include

- Walking away
- Saying "It's private"
- *Sharing.* "She did want me, but she wasn't able to take care of me at the time. I Skyped with her last night and got to see my new baby brother."
- *Educating.* "Do you mean my birth mom? She loves me very much. She tells me so a lot, every time I see her."
- *Questioning.* "Why do you want to know?"

- *Deflecting.* "That's a boring topic. Catch this ball!"
- *Using humor.* "Oh, my real mom loves me a lot. It's my fake mom I'm worried about."

You will have plenty of chances to learn this assessment and reaction yourself and model it to your child. As we've said, the more comfortable we are in our own stories, the less it matters to us what anyone else thinks.

ROOTS AND BRANCHES

Inevitably the child will have a school assignment to draw a family tree. When this arises, rather than causing confusion it can be a cause for celebration: "Look how many loving people there are in this tree—I have roots and branches and leaves. I have more leaves than I can count!"

Of course, a tree is simply the default option for conceptualizing one's family. But it's not the only way. Alternatives include

- *Roots and branches.* Birth-family members are listed as roots, and adoptive family members are listed in the branches, or vice versa
- *Family houses.* A network of houses that contain people connected to the child by biology or biography
- *The family wheel.* The child at the center, parents around the first ring, siblings in the second ring, grandparents in the next ring, working outward
- *And others.* A good resource for the family-tree assignment in school is on *Adoptive Families* magazine's website.[3]

Andy, an adult adoptee and adoptive mama, describes on her blog, *Today's the Day They Give Babies Away*, how she felt when a teacher pulled out the family-tree assignment and what she now advocates in her son's classroom:

> The main issue is that the standard tree format does not have any space to include first-family information. And there are, of course, other issues about this project.

The first big question is, *Do I want to share with the class that I am adopted?* Every time something new came up like this, I had to reexamine how much I wanted to share. Once a kid decides that she is going to share the fact that she was adopted, the problem becomes the format. Most schools send home a printout sheet of a tree that needs to be filled in. That leaves the adoptee the option to pencil in her first family info or create her own format.

There are lots of formats available to use, but for me that didn't solve the base problem. What kid wants to be the only one in class whose sheet looks different?

The best idea, it seems, is to leave the project open-ended and let each kid decide how to present it. That way each child can choose whom to include, how much to include, and how she wants to display it. This works not just for adoptees but for kids with single parents; kids with families who have divorced, remarried, and added step- or half-siblings to the mix; and every other family type that happens in today's world. Kids can include Auntie So-and-So, who isn't really an aunt but one of the most important people in that child's life. No one gets singled out, and the true spirit of the project is accomplished.[4]

With all of today's options in family building, and with all the permutations and combinations that can take place in a family unit, this adoptee and mama is right: adaptability is key in this project. Andy approached her son's teacher with these insights, and the teacher was pleased to change the assignment to be more child directed. Allowing the child to control what information is shared and how is highly empowering.

ONE FAMILY, MORE THAN ONE ADOPTION

Unfairness, imbalance, and inequity are easy for children to spot and difficult for them to tolerate. When one child in a family has less openness with first parents, or when there are biological children in the family, issues may arise.

For seven years, my son, Reed, had no contact with his birth dad and very little contact with his birth mom. By contrast, my daughter, Tessa, had a very present birth mother as well as a birth father who joined our extended family when Tessa was seven and Reed was five.

There was very little we could do to fix the imbalance. We could not make Reed's birth mom respond to the voice-mail messages he'd leave for her. We didn't know enough information about his birth father to find him, nor did we know what his demeanor and intentions would be if we did. Cutting back contact with Tessa's first families seemed wrong, too: staying away from Crystal and Joe might have eased Reed's longing but would likely have caused new problems for Tessa.

Instead, we dealt with what we had. From the day we brought Reed home, Crystal treated him as a child equal to Tessa in her eyes. If she showed up with a Hello Kitty purse for Tessa, she'd also have a foam sword for Reed. If she held a party for her son, both Tessa's and Reed's names were on the invitation.

When Joe, Tessa's first father, came into our lives, we made sure he knew that the kids were a package deal. And, being a caring and compassionate person, he understood our reasoning. When Joe called to talk with Tessa on the phone, he often also asked to speak with Reed. Both children were greeted warmly when we'd meet at a playground or for dinner. And, fortunately, Joe has a stepson who is Reed's age, so Reed was happily occupied whenever we met up.

None of this contact with Tessa's birth parents fooled Reed or replaced the contact he lacked with his own birth parents, but at his developmental stage it definitely soothed.

There were a few nights when Reed cried at bedtime, lamenting the fact that his own birth mother was present only in a photograph. At times like this I did not tell him it was okay. I did not point out what he did have in Crystal or in me. I did not say I'm sure his birth mother loved him anyway. I did not gloss over his pain.

I sat with it. I breathed with him. I held him. I gave him space and support to grieve and feel sad. Remarkably, Reed did not get stuck in the sadness. And, eventually, his birth father surfaced and eagerly built a relationship with his birth son. His birth mom has also popped into our lives on occasion.

PARENTING BY BIRTH AND ADOPTION

Another perceived imbalance can exist in families that have children through biology and via adoption. One prospective adoptive mom, Alicia, finally became pregnant after struggling with infertility and miscarriage for years; this surprise natural pregnancy coincided with an adoption match. To avoid being "greedy," Alicia and her husband, James, told the expectant mother who had chosen them that she was free to choose another couple to parent her baby.

Just a month after their son, Hunter, was born, he died unexpectedly. Alicia and James didn't think anything more of the adoption as they grieved their son. After all, time had passed, and surely the baby had found a stable home, one way or another. Alicia says, "Shortly after Hunter's funeral, I got a call out of the blue from the woman we'd matched with. I hadn't had any contact with her, and I assumed her baby had been placed with a new family. She related to me that she'd heard about Hunter and she was sorry and that if I still wanted Hayden he was sitting in foster care."

Instead of completing a designated adoption, Alicia and James now wended their way through the foster-care system and eventually became parents to Hayden. Two years later, Alicia had another unexpected pregnancy, and their daughter, Ashley, was born when Hayden was two-and-a-half years old.

The topic of adoption has come up in the intervening years. One day when Hayden was seven and Ashley was five, the family drove by the office of Alicia's OB/GYN.

> I told Ashley, "That's where mommy was all the time when you were in my tummy," and Hayden said, "Why wasn't I in your tummy again?" I told him because a nice lady had him in *her* tummy but that when he was born she didn't think she had a nice enough home for him and she wanted more for him, so she asked us to take him home and love him and be his family. Hayden thought for a second, then said, "Yeah, she probably didn't have a TV."[5]

Ah, kids.

Hayden's response underscores how literal children can be. While Alicia meant stability and sustenance when she said "nice home," Hayden heard "a building with stuff in it I like."

Alicia says of questions her children might ask her in the future about their different origins, "I am a big believer in communication with my kids, and so I like to think I would answer any questions they have or that if I don't know the answer I will try to find it for them."

When asked how she will know what to say, where her answers to questions about adoption will come from, Alicia says, "I just try to be mindful of seeing things through their eyes rather than through my adult eyes."[6]

CRYSTAL SAYS: When Tessa was ten, she asked me why I made the decision I did: "Why was I adopted?" First, I think it's helpful to her that she was able to come to the source to find out.

And, second, in the conversation we had I can see how well she is healing any split that adoption may have caused.

"It wasn't that I couldn't take care of you," I told her. "It was that I was afraid for the security of both of us and Tyler [my parented son] if you and I had stayed together. As you know, at that time the dynamics between Joe and me were not good. But I wanted you, and I knew I would have been a good mom to you, and I wanted to be your mom. Very much."

"Crystal," said Tessa, "If I'd stayed with you, then I would have a huge hole in my heart for my mom and dad."

"But, honey," I told her, "you wouldn't even know them."

"But you know how you know someone belongs with you, like my Teddy [bear]? And you know how you know when you're just missing something? That's how it would be if I weren't with my mom and dad."

CLOSED ADOPTION AND THE ADOPTEE

People who were adopted in the 1940s, 1950s, 1960s, 1970s, and 1980s likely grew up in closed adoptions. During the Baby-Scoop Era, a pregnancy that occurred outside of marriage brought stigma to the mother and to the child. Because of the shame, many expectant mothers were shipped to homes for unwed mothers and their babies were whisked away after the birth. The mother was expected to move on as if nothing had happened. It was assumed that the infant, seen as a blank slate, would suffer no effects of being brought into a new family, that nurture clearly trumped nature.

Nancy Verrier, author of the groundbreaking *Primal Wound: Understanding the Adopted Child*, says that the theory of the baby as a blank slate "ignores one simple but critical fact. *The adoptee was there.*"[7]

Some children adopted during the Baby-Scoop Era never wanted to seek out their birth parents. Some began searching when they came of age, some later in life. Some of them found the names of their birth parents, some actually met their birth parents, and some found the graves of their birth parents. Some reunions went well, some went sour, and some didn't go at all. Some adoptees reached dead end after dead end during their searches, thwarted by sealed records and amended birth certificates, walls that still keep adults from accessing their personal documents in many states today.

Parents embarking on an adoption journey can learn a lot about emotions their own children may experience by listening to adult adoptees on various points of the contentedness spectrum. Here is Maggie's story.

"IT WAS A THRILL"

Maggie Macaulay was a child adopted in the 1950s. She came into a family that already had a biological son, Maggie's older brother. Maggie later gained a younger brother through adoption.

> I was always curious about my birth mother and the circumstances of my adoption. My mother shared all that she knew. She did not attempt to make up things or fill in the blanks where she did not have the information. Adoption was always viewed as something wonderful and normal. There was not, however, the recognition and acceptance of the importance of a child having her birth information back then as there is now. I always felt that my mother believed that asking about my birth mother or showing too much curiosity meant she had not done a good job as a mother—that she believed that I would not be curious if she was a good enough mother. I felt disenfranchised from my biological history because it was not viewed as meaningful information. This was not an intentionally malicious or

hurtful thing but more the way of the culture back then. People did not know how to deal with the ambiguities and complexities of adoption.[8]

Wouldn't it be normal for any kid to wonder about her biological roots—or at least not abnormal? To wonder what one's life might have been like if things had gone another way? If my own children do not feel free to wonder and think about their birth parents and about the lives they might have lived, that disallowance might create dark spots in their psyches, unexplored places that become scary because of the darkness. I want them to be able to shine light on whatever they need to as they cognitively process their birth stories and their adoptedness.

Maggie, now of Whole Hearted Parenting, tells about her search for her roots.

As an adult I requested nonidentifying information from the agency that handled the adoption. I later requested identifying information and found a few birth-family members. My birth mother had died in 1974 of breast cancer—the number of birth mothers who die of breast cancer is statistically high. I have talked with birth-family members on the telephone, and we exchange Christmas cards. They were very welcoming, providing me with photographs and items that had belonged to my birth mother. It was a thrill to look at photographs of her and see features that we share.[9]

LOOKING IN THE MIRROR

Nonadopted people may take for granted the fact that we grow up looking into faces that are biologically connected to us. I grew up knowing that I looked like others in my household—my sisters and my parents (I didn't see the resemblance, but others told me it was there). Now, as I watch my parents' faces and bodies age, I have a good idea what I'm in for. When I see a facial expression on one of my sisters, I know I probably have it, too. It's like having walking mirrors, at times.

Jenn Lawlor is an adult adoptee recently reunited with her birth father. In her blog post "Looking in the mirror," she explains how strange it is to see someone else in her face for the first time in her life.

I know [now] that my facial structure comes from my first father and my first mother. I've always loved my eyes, but now there's another reason why I love them. When I met my first father, the first thing I noticed was that he has the exact same eyes as me. It's like looking in the mirror. What an odd feeling. Now when I look in the mirror I see that history there. I see my heritage and my biological family reflected in my face. I know this is a huge reason why I want to meet my first mother, so that I can see for myself our similarities.[10]

THE "REAL" CONUNDRUM

Torrejon, born in the 1960s, explains the ridiculousness that the word *real* evokes in her and how having all her parental pieces would help her be made whole:

> If you ask someone who has four kids, *Which one is your real child? The one who looks like you? The one who was named after you? The one you've had the longest? The one who shares your love of [insert passion here]?*, people understand how crazy the question is.
> But people just don't understand how I can have four parents. If I want to ask a question about my genetics, one of my birth parents would be my best source. If I want to ask about a childhood memory, my adoptive parents are going to be the best source.
> It's just common sense. I'm not going to ask my dad about make-up tips, and I'm not going to ask my mom to look at the brakes on my car. Correct source equals correct answers.[11]

HERITAGE AND IDENTITY IN THE TEEN YEARS

In 1995 an Australian study by Pete Westwood made the following points about adolescents and identify formation:

- Determining identity is a difficult enough process for someone brought up by their natural parents; it is even more complex for those whose ancestry is unknown to them.
- The more information that adopted adolescents have about their biological parents and the circumstances of their relinquishment,

the more easily they can establish a basis from which identity formation and integration can take place.

- The absence of knowledge of past origins and the concern about a family identity can lead to genealogical bewilderment. This bewilderment can be triggered in adolescence or later in life by developmental crisis points and environmental stresses such as illness, marriage, pregnancy, divorce, or the death of adoptive parents.

- The majority of reunions with natural parents strengthen, rather than weaken, the adoptee's feelings toward the adoptive parents. Adoptees want to be able to say to their adoptive parents, "Help me find myself and my [birth] parents so that I will know who I am."

- Adoptees, generally, are not distinguishable from the population at large, and presumptions should not be made that all will have similar dilemmas to work through. However, sensitivity to the problems of identity in adolescence in general, and among adoptees in particular, will benefit those young people who are trying resolve the very real question of who they are.[12]

Alex Haley explored ancestry in the 1970s, and the country became hooked on *Roots*. Amateur genealogists do it in their spare time, devoting countless hours to discovering who they are, based on who came before them and what lives were lived. A television show was formed on it, NBC's *Who Do You Think You Are?*, because people are fascinated by their origins. Why would we not allow our children the same luxury, to indulge that inner yearning to know, to wonder about their genetic roots?

We do a disservice to the adopted person when we try to establish a hierarchy between nature and nurture. If our own insecurities require us to assert that nurture is more important than nature, then perhaps we should dissolve those insecurities rather than discount a person's biology.

Biology and biography do coexist and can do so peacefully when we acknowledge and honor both. In doing so we help our children reintegrate what was split at the moment of placement and we give them a better chance of growing up whole.

WHEN CONTACT ISN'T POSSIBLE

Even when parents want to provide birth-parent contact for their children, there are many reasons why it may not be possible: distance, death, mental illness, safety issues, incarceration, to name a few. Is all hope lost, then, for a child's healthy identity formation in these situations?

Not at all. We've said before that openness isn't just something we do, it's what we believe and the way we behave with our children. It's in the spirit of how we talk about their first families and how we think of adoption in general.

A 2011 study published in the *Journal of Family Psychology* shows that it may not be just *contact* that helps the teen integrate his identities but also the *conversation* about contact—*the being open to openness*—that helps. "Adoptive parents' facilitation of contact," the researchers reported, "creates opportunities for them to talk with their children about adoption." In fact, one of the authors had previously learned that

> warm and supportive interactions between parents and adolescents, in which children are encouraged to express their views and ideas, are associated with higher levels of adolescent identity exploration across domains including occupational choice, ideology, and relationships. The extent to which conversation is helpful to an emerging sense of self . . . and to adoptees' psychological adjustment depends on open communication about adoption . . . and conversational styles.[13]

OPEN RECORDS: A CIVIL RIGHTS ISSUE

By now you're probably surmising that openness means many things in adoption. It means open contact or openness *to* contact. It means open communication within the adoption constellation. It means being open to and not closing down emotions that may arise. It means being open to possibilities, to being vulnerable.

It should also mean opening records for adopted people.

My husband and I are in possession of two birth certificates for each of our children. The original documents were registered at the time of their births and have the name each child was given by their original mothers in the hospital, as well as the names of their original mothers (but not fathers, which is a whole different issue). The second or *amended* birth certificates were issued at the time each adoption was finalized, when our children were six or seven months old, respectively, and have my husband's and my names on them. My children are luckier than some other adopted people—as adults they will have full access to their own birth records.

Not so for all adoptees. In all except seven states there are adult citizens who, because of circumstances of their birth and subsequent adoption, are not currently able to have their own original birth certificates. Some of the remaining forty-three states do allow limited access but require high fees or the intervention of court-appointed intermediaries who are granted permission by the court of jurisdiction to open sealed records for the purpose of the search—or not. Nonadopted people can have unimpeded access to their birth certificates, yet adopted people cannot, which is what makes this a civil-rights issue.

The reason usually given for nonaccess is that birth mothers were promised privacy, especially during the Baby-Scoop Era.[14] But let's look more deeply at the reasons for this policy and its effects on adoptees.

MYTH #1: ADOPTEE BIRTH CERTIFICATES ARE SEALED TO PROTECT BIRTH-PARENT PRIVACY

If the practice of sealing birth records were really about protecting the privacy of the birth mother, then records would be sealed at the time of *relinquishment*. Yet this is not the case. You see, records are sealed only when an adoption is *finalized*, indicating that the original intent was not to prevent people from identifying a birth mother but, perhaps, to protect the adoptive parents from pesky birth parents or to protect the adopted child from the "shame" of adoption or possibly to protect the adoption agency from being held accountable for adhering to ethical and moral standards. A child who is relinquished but never adopted would always have full access to his original birth records, his birth mother always clearly identified. So, obviously, the policy was never about protecting birth-parent privacy.

The New Jersey Coalition for Adoption Reform and Education (NJCARE) is an organization dedicated to unsealing birth records for all citizens in New Jersey. According to it,

> neither the U.S. Constitution nor the N.J. statute defines privacy as a right of a parent to remain unknown to their offspring. . . . Birth parents have no "constitutional right to anonymity." Birth parents do not sign a contract guaranteeing them anonymity or a right to privacy. There can be no right, morally or constitutionally, to conceal the fact of parentage from one's own child. If there were such a right, how could paternity suits be allowed? In fact, the law has recognized paternity suits for centuries. Why does the law give relinquishing birth mothers the right to hide from their children but withhold that right from fathers who chose not to parent?[15]

MYTH #2: BAD THINGS WILL HAPPEN IF RECORDS ARE OPENED

You might think that birth parents in the seven states that have no barriers would report being stalked and having their lives disrupted by adoptees using birth documents to track them down. You might think that if it were so awful for placing parents to be forced to identify themselves then abortion rates would be higher in these states. You might think social havoc has been wreaked in these states and its citizens would be clamoring to pass laws revoking access.

And you would be wrong.

In a 2010 paper, the Donaldson Adoption Institute found that "the experiences of many other countries, of U.S. states where birth certificates have never been sealed from adopted persons, and of those states that have restored access all indicate that there are few if any problems when access is granted."[16]

MYTH #3: IN SOME STATES, SOME ADULT ADOPTEES CAN ACCESS THEIR BIRTH RECORDS AND OTHERS CAN'T

Believe it or not, sensible or not, this myth is true. Some states are called *blackout states* because they have passed laws that, based on the date of the adoption finalization, grant some adoptees access and prevent others from getting their original birth certificates. How does the State of Colorado, for example, justify releasing a birth certificate to someone whose adoption was finalized on June 30, 1967, but not to the person whose adoption was finalized just one day later?[17]

THE IMPACT OF SEALED RECORDS ON DRIVER'S LICENSES

If your daughter grows up, moves to, say, South Carolina, and wants to get a driver's license but doesn't have access to her birth records, she could be in for a difficult time of it. South Carolina's Department of Motor Vehicles states that "if your name has changed since birth, you must provide all legal documents (adoption records, marriage certificate, certificate of naturalization, court-ordered name change) supporting all name changes from birth to present."[18] And, yes, South Carolina is a sealed-record state: "The original birth certificate is placed in a special sealed file by the state registrar. The statute does not specify a procedure for access to the original certificate."[19] And to further confuse the issue, some jurisdictions—not only in South Carolina but in other states as well—do not recognize the legitimacy of amended birth certificates.

THE IMPACT OF SEALED RECORDS ON PASSPORTS

Had your son passed his first birthday by the time his amended birth certificate was filed? Then he may have difficulty one day acquiring a U.S. passport. The State Department requires that a citizen present a certified birth certificate that shows the date of filing with the registrar's office within one year of the birth.[20] If your son cannot get his original birth certificate, in this case he won't be able to meet U.S. passport requirements with his amended birth certificate. And if you're like my friend Jeni who has three possible birthdays, because the state of New York has three different birth records for her, none of them "original," you wouldn't even know when the one-year clock started ticking in the first place.

THE IMPACT OF SEALED RECORDS THROUGH THE GENERATIONS

Another friend, Juli, tells me that one of the worst things about having been adopted is going to the doctor. She is always asked about her health history—including her parents' and grandparents'—in order to assess her risk factors. She draws a blank each and every time. She has no clue if the physical and medical experiences she's had are rooted in her genetic makeup, her unknown ethnic heritage.

But being denied her information isn't just bad news for Juli; her children and grandchildren will also have big gaps in the knowledge of their medical and genealogical histories.

Closed records are the gift that keeps on taking, generation after generation.

Because opening records for all is a state issue, it cannot be resolved through federal legislation in one fell swoop. The Adoptee Rights Coalition (ARC) holds a demonstration each summer that coincides with the annual meeting of the National Conference of State Legislators. Theirs is a campaign to raise awareness among lawmakers in nonopen states about a civil-rights issue that remains for one class of citizens. ARC's efforts, coupled with changing public opinion, could very well mean that current laws sealing original birth certificates will be successfully challenged and overturned in your child's lifetime.[21]

And why should every adoptive parent care about this mess? Because even though *you* may have access to your child's original birth certificate, not everyone does. This means that your child is a member of a class of people whose rights are not fully recognized. When children are small, it can be difficult to imagine that they will one day become autonomous adults. Yet they do, and no competent adult should be safeguarded from access to an accurate record of birth by any parent or agency, especially not when nonadopted citizens are not treated the same way. Allowing universal access to one's personal records should matter in open adoptions, in international adoptions, in foster adoption, in all adoptions. *All* parents involved in adoption should care about transparency and openness so that ethical practice in adoptions is assured (or, in the case of past unethical practices, exposed). We owe this to our children.

MOVING FORWARD

We've heard from adult adoptees about how it feels to grow up in a closed adoption, how it feels to be split or incomplete, how it feels to be presented with an uncomfortable school assignment, and how they might deal with well-meaning and possibly ill-meaning inquisitors. We've touched on both the importance of contact with birth family and the helpfulness of the *openness to being open* when contact is not possible. We've addressed the issue of open records and how it is our responsibility as parents to make sure our children have their inherent rights recognized.

On the next leg of our trip we'll look at some intimate parenting moments—parenting wins on the road to wholeness.

6

HEADING TOWARD WHOLENESS: INTEGRATING YOUR CHILD'S BIOLOGY AND BIOGRAPHY

There is no *there* there.[1] Your son or daughter will be heading toward wholeness for as long as he or she lives. Your job as the parent is to point your child in the right direction and offer the tools, support, and encouragement to make the journey.

To know where we want this journey to take us, we must be able to visualize that destination. And so in this chapter we devote ourselves to understanding what healthy integration and identity formation looks like in a child who was adopted. We'll cover otherness, and we'll talk further about moving from an either/or mind-set to an and/both mind-set. We'll talk about reunion *within* an open adoption (not as oxymoronic as it sounds). We'll discuss birth-family relationships beyond the first mom and first dad. And throughout we will share some conversations showing how children process their adoptedness at various stages, offering us glimpses into the integration of their biology and biography.

A FAIRY TALE MADE FOR ADOPTIVE FAMILIES

In 1843 Hans Christian Anderson published a fairy tale that has resonated with readers ever since. The story of "The Ugly Duckling" explores a theme most of us can relate to at one time or another—the idea of not fitting in. And the resonance can be especially strong for children who grow up adopted.

Judy M. Miller, author of *What to Expect from Your Adopted Tween*, has written an insightful blog post in which she likens the tale to what is required of those who parent via adoption:

> Remember the story of "The Ugly Duckling," in which a baby swan was hatched and raised by a duck? The mother duck could teach the ugly duckling everything there was to being a duck, but she couldn't teach him about being a swan.
>
> The baby swan was perceived as an outsider and, therefore, believed he was ugly. He didn't realize he was a beautiful swan until he was an adult, but he had already suffered so much.
>
> The story of "The Ugly Duckling" is about how a creature feels when he is not connected to his birth heritage or culture . . . [it] is a tale about a swan in search of his place and his identity.
>
> Upon reading "The Ugly Duckling" to my children, I took away a deeper message as an adoptive parent. The story of the ugly duckling is similar to adoption and what needs to happen within the adoptive family.
>
> One of the biggest challenges as an adoptive parent, especially as a parent to internationally and transracially adopted children, is that I cannot address all of their needs, specifically the desire to know and understand their birth culture first-hand. Like the ugly duckling, each of my children is in search of self, their identity. I can teach my kids about being the duck—sharing my history and heritage, what it is to be part of our family, and what it means to be an American. And I can share our values and beliefs with them.
>
> How my kids feel, what they think about adoption, their races, ethnicities, and birth cultures is important to me. *I can't teach them what it means to be a swan, because I'm a duck.* Heritage and culture are lived. *But I can offer them opportunities to become as familiar and embrace their birth cultures.* I can guide and support each child as they work toward discovering and creating their identities, including any search for birth parents/family members [emphasis added].
>
> While my children search for themselves, it is imperative that they do not feel like an outsider but feel that they belong, that they matter to us and to each other. Each of my children understands that they hold a special and unique place within our family and are deeply loved.[2]

Judy makes the case that our children should not feel ugly because they are surrounded by otherness, whether that otherness comes via international, transracial, or transfamilial adoption. This doesn't mean we should discourage our children from noticing their differentness, however. They do notice differences in skin tone and hair color, variances in formation of teeth and the set of the eyes, dissimilarities in body build, not to mention differences in personality, temperament, and innate talents. If we try to convince them that differences aren't noticeable or don't matter, we only dull their observation skills, because differences *are* noticeable and sometimes *do* matter. Instead, we must show our children how to deal with how things *are* rather than with how we wish things were.

REED: MY SON DEALS WITH OTHERNESS AT SCHOOL

My towheaded son and I were confronted with our differences one day in his classroom.

"Your mom doesn't look like you at *all*," said the second grader to my son.

From my perch on a chair much too small for my bottom, I looked at the girl's desk to find out her name, written in teacher-tidy print. Joy.

"That's 'cause she a-*dopted* me," Reed told his classmate across the table.

And that's how Take-Your-Parent-to-School Day began.

Now I knew, in the abstract, that school presented new challenges for adoptees to navigate. I just didn't know, really *know*, that such challenges would be presented to *my* children.

And the exchange was over before I even saw it coming. I was secretly pleased at my son's choice of words: Did you notice he didn't say, "That's 'cause I'm adopted"? He said, "*That's 'cause she adopted me.*"

It's a subtle difference. I have always hoped that my children would see adoption as a word to describe what their parents *did* rather than who they *were*. Verb versus adjective, not self-definition.

But is that a distinction that we adoptive parents cling to, shoehorning space between the two phrases just to make us feel like we're doing something right by using sensitive and sensible language? Or, as some adoptees say, does it matter not a whit? Tomayto/tomahto, was adopted/is adopted? Some adoptees have told me being adopted *is* who they are. And some have said it's just one part of who they are. I have no way of knowing where, on a continuum of adoption identity, my child is hardwired to be, but I can encourage him to openly work it out with me. It's an earned privilege to be trusted with his innermost thoughts.

"Why do you think Joy said that?" I whispered to Reed later as the class walked single-file to Library.

"I dunno," he shrugged. "Maybe because your hair is darker than mine."

"What do you think of that?" I probed.

"I think people have different hair."

We arrived at the library, and that was that.

Reed had clearly noticed that I had brown hair and he had blond hair. I could not have told him otherwise and been believed. I could not have told him that hair color doesn't matter and remained credible—someone had just noticed we looked different. What I *could* do was be comfortable myself with the fact that we don't share the same hair color and simply ask Reed questions to find out if I sensed anything for him to process. My line of questioning revealed that he, too, was comfortable with our having different hair and talking about his adoption. I did not insert any of my own issues into the conversation that took place on the way to the school library.

We help our children form and integrate their identities when we enable them to connect, directly or indirectly, with their clan of birth—parents, extended family, or group of heritage—so that they are able to incorporate their very beingness (swanness) into their sense of identity. The ugly duckling wasn't able to do so while dwelling exclusively with ducks. The identity incorporation happened only during the aha moment when he realized his swanness

This is why in an open adoption, in which all involved parents have the child's well-being as a focal point, it can be very helpful, in situations in which it's possible, for a child to spend time with his or her biological parents or family or clan. Doing so need not take anything away from the adoptive family. Doing so simply adds to the child.

TESSA: RETURNING TO THE WELL

When Tessa was six years old, we faced a new first: Crystal had offered to take both of my children for the afternoon. Since the very beginning, Crystal had attended birthday parties for both Tessa and Reed and had come to school events and dance recitals, averaging about a visit a month. But up until that point I'd always been part of the get-togethers.

I had to sit with my thoughts and feelings about leaving my children with Tessa's birth mom. I went through my mental checklist.

Would my children be safe? Yes. Was I worried that I'd be usurped as Mom? No. Could Crystal handle both my children, in addition to her own? Yes. Might my son feel left out? That question was also easily dismissed; Crystal had always shown her love for Reed, and Reed got along well with Crystal's ten-year-old son.

I decided there was no reason not to proceed. I drove the kids to Crystal's house, cautioned them to behave, reminded Crystal that she could call me, no matter what, and left, almost giddy at the open space and time ahead of me.

When I returned four hours later to pick up the children, Crystal had trimmed Tessa's hair and given her a pair of hand-me-down purple spiked boots. I reported that I'd I spent my quiet hours of solitude reading, and they told me that they had spent their loud hours of togetherness running through the sprinkler and eating. We were all fulfilled.

Now, let me expand a bit on my relationship with Tessa at that time. She and I would butt heads over everything from how long she spent in the shower to doing her homework (yes—in kindergarten!), from how long she spent talking on the phone to doing her chores. I feared what the coming years might look like if already when she was six we were locking horns over issues that only get more complex in the teen years. Back then, it seemed Tessa and I "missed" each other often. I was frustrated with our disconnect, and I imagined Tessa was, too. I felt like the duck to her swan.

When we got home from Crystal's, Tessa said, "Mom, I'm a new person!" I wasn't sure if she meant the new hairstyle, the baptism-by-sprinkler, or something less identifiable. But for days afterward, the prickliness in her was gone. The morning after the visit with her birth mom, Tessa wanted to wear the spiky purple boots to kindergarten. "Those shoes are not appropriate for school," I warned her. Pressing her to think ahead, I advised her, "You do what you think will get you the consequences you want." I half-expected her to wear the ill-fitting boots to school, which would have meant I'd have to give them away (in our household, items that cause disharmony go away).

But Tessa came to breakfast, smiling and cheerful, wearing her sneakers. I was so impressed with her response that I brought the boots when I picked her up from school so she could wear them to the dentist, which was a more appropriate place than the schoolyard for a kid to play dress-up.

After her time with Crystal, it was as if Tessa had been to the well. You see, I'd realized that my temperament doesn't always align with hers. I'm orderly and analytical. She's is mercurial and playful—traits she shares with her first mom. But seeing my daughter's deep satisfaction made me think that maybe spending time with Crystal is, for Tessa, like sinking into a comfortable chair.

Should I feel hurt or threatened by Crystal's positive effect on Tessa? I don't, and here's why.

I don't know how to fix a tooth, but I *can* take Tessa to Dr. Jill. I don't like to play house for hours at a time, but I *can* invite Tessa's friends for a visit. I'm ill-equipped to teach Tessa gymnastics, but I *can* arrange for lessons with Miss Amber. And I can't fill a certain emotional need that Tessa has, but I *can* take her to the well.

Doing so serves us all.

FROM EITHER/OR TO AND/BOTH

We easily recognize the dual nature of our world: day/night, good/bad, male/female, light/dark, black/white. It's the nuances, the shades of gray, that are difficult to discern and incorporate into our thinking. But the more we integrate them, the more we move toward unity and wholeness. Perhaps nowhere more so than in adoption.

Adoption creates a split in a person between his biology and his biography. Openness in adoption is an effective way to heal that split.

For most of the twentieth century, adoption culture spoke in terms of the either/or: either you are the "real" dad or another man is. Your daughter's love and loyalty must be directed at either you or him. When speak this way, we may not realize it, but we are splitting the baby, continuing to rend their biological and biographical stories.

And who says it has to be that way? Question that very fundamental thought. Why not *and*? Why not *both*? Making such a shift in your thinking does not require you to give up anything. There is enough love and enough space in your daughter's heart for both you and her other father. Your child will be looking to you for cues that this is true, for permission to love all parts of herself.

And this integration doesn't mean there's anything for you to *do*; rather, it offers a new way for you to think and believe. Because the more you can incorporate a focus on abundance, on And, the more easily your daughter will be able to, as well. When she gets it that opening up to her birth dad does't mean withholding anything from you, she will not fear losing you.

Now put yourself in my son's shoes, and feel the difference between these two options:

1. *Either/Or.* "Go ahead, Reed, try to decide which set of parents you love more. Put us first and those other people in their place. If the house were on fire and you could save only one set of us, which would it be?" Would this not be like asking Reed to cut out one of his organs?
2. *And/Both.* "Michele and AJ, your birth parents, are important to you in one way, Reed, and Daddy and I are important in another. Of course you would love both sets of us, all of us."

Encouraging our son to have ample room for all four of us in his heart is much less torturous and more integrating than forcing him to rank us or choose between us.

As Torrejon said back in chapter 5, we acknowledge that parents are capable of loving multiple children. So why not allow—*encourage*—children to do the same with multiple parents?

TESSA: THE PUSH AND PULL OF ADOPTION REUNION

Tessa's birthfather, Joe, didn't come into our lives right away. Crystal had told us that Joe was too volatile, too unpredictable, to be in our lives. But seven years can mellow a person. Crystal and Joe had continued intermittent contact with each other after Tessa was born, but after a time each ended up moving on to another relationship.

Eventually Crystal told us that if we wanted to contact Joe she would put us in touch. My husband and I exchanged e-mails with Joe, and, after an online courtship, the three of us decided to meet—just the adults—with facilitation by our adoption agency. Roger and I wanted to determine whether or not it would be safe to introduce Tessa to her birth father.

We needn't have worried. Joe was sincere and straightforward. He started the meeting by telling us that he didn't expect anything from us and that he was glad we'd come. He explained that the birth of his daughter, Ivy, the year before had stirred painful emotions about Tessa. We exchanged photos. We talked. We agreed that the next step would be for Joe to meet Tessa later that summer.

The next day, Tessa noticed my flopped-open purse, with the pictures of Joe and his daughter in it. I've been a mom long enough to know not to tell a child that something is going to happen until it is practically happening, so I hadn't planned on telling Tessa about him yet. I braced myself for her response.

"Mommy, can I see those pictures?" I handed them over. "Who is he? And is this cute baby me?"

"No, Sweetheart. This man is Joe, your birth father. Daddy and I met him yesterday to make sure that it was all right to have him in our lives."

"Really? So what did you talk about?"

"He was curious about you. He has always loved you and wondered about you."

"I want to meet him, too, Mom."

"That's great, because he also wants to meet you. But with all our trips coming up, and Joe's schedule, we're going to have to wait until later in the summer."

I handled the conversation well, but now Tessa would have to endure a two-month wait. We tried to keep a positive outlook. We hoped that Tessa and Joe could get to know each other over the phone first and ease into a relationship. This was not, however, to be the case.

Tessa and Joe began exchanging phone calls two or three times a week. Joe always chatted with my husband or me first and then asked if it were okay to talk with Tessa. I was thankful that he thought about Tessa's needs and also that he often asked to speak with Reed, as well, respecting and accepting that we are a package deal.

Tessa was giddy with each phone call. She felt very special. Perhaps she had in her mind that Joe was a person who would "fix" whatever was wrong with her life—*he* would surely give her a set of real keys (she loved real keys, indicators of power); *he* would take her swimming every day because he has a pool *right near his house*; *he* would let her stay up as late as she wanted.

So she had this *pull* toward him.

My job, as I saw it, was to keep her grounded amid her fantasy. She was very mad at me during this time. We continued to have chores, bedtimes, rules, and limits.

But one day I became aware of Tessa's *push* away from Joe. And I can't believe I hadn't noticed it before. I'd been so intent on providing her the freedom to develop a relationship with her birth dad that I had almost missed something crucial.

One afternoon Tessa and I had an out-of-proportion argument over a chore. She went from zero to steam-coming-out-the-ears in a flash. Her eyes a-blazing, she hissed, "And if I don't, are you going to send me to Joe?"

What?

Sudden flash of insight: She wasn't *just* worried that we would keep her from meeting Joe. She was *also* worried that we might abdicate our place as her parents. This thought, I believe, filled her with terror. Like an earthquake was about to hit.

"Oh, Sweetie." I came toward her, and she collapsed into my arms, her flame doused by her tears. "Do you think Daddy and I would ever let you go? We will *always* be your parents, no matter what. We love you *no matter what*. Now you just have someone else in your life who also loves you and who wants good things for you."

I continued, "Your life won't change a lot when you meet Joe. This is your home. Reed is your brother. Daddy and I will always tuck you in at night and wake you up in the morning."

"Teddy [Bear] and my babies will always be mine?"

"Yes," I said. And smiled, "And you'll still have to eat your veggies and empty the trash and finish your homework and kiss your mother!" as I smooched the air at her and tickled her.

Her body relaxed.

I am still chastened by the fact that I hadn't recognized the push/pull in Tessa as it emerged and tried to mitigate it. Fortunately Tessa is resilient and strong, traits she'll call on again and again.

LAYING THE GROUNDWORK: TALKING ABOUT ADOPTION WITH YOUR KIDS

In my early days of parenting I read everything I could find about best practices. I read *Adoptive Families* magazine. I lurked on adoption forums. I talked with friends I'd met at adoption school. I picked the brain of our adoption social worker. I checked out adoption books from the library. I sought viewpoints of others involved in adoption, both offline and online, in international and domestic and foster adoptions, in open and closed adoptions. And from all this I gleaned some key ideas that my husband and I put into practice when broaching the topic of adoption with our two kids.

- *Start as early as possible.* Our agency suggested we tell our infant daughter the story of how she came to be our daughter. I thought that was ridiculous: She was years from being able to understand. She was a newborn, for goodness' sake.

  Then I realized that getting comfortable with the story wasn't for our *child's* benefit—it was for ours. Now I firmly believe that the more Roger and I accept all that led Tessa to our family—the painful parts as well as the joyous parts—the more at ease she will be with her story.

  One great complement to any adoption story is Jamie Lee Curtis's *Tell Me Again about the Night I Was Born*. This book has so much, visually, for a child to notice and laugh about, and laughing is very effective when conversing about these tough topics.[3]

- *Kids are literal. Very, very literal.* Let's say you tell your son he was born from your heart. One day he inevitably grasps how births actually happen, and now you have sent him on an anatomical wild-goose chase as he tries to envision exactly how he could have been born from your heart. Literally, born from your heart. Although it's a nice sentiment, wait to use such phrasing until he's able to understand nuance, metaphor, analogies, figures of speech—probably at least age ten.

• *Have a series of little talks* so you can avoid the shock that can come from The Big Talk. This will work better for you as well as for your child, because the emotional charge and the topic's bigness will be spread out over time.

• *All babies are born.* Remember to point out that your child was born the same way nonadopted children are. No babies are hatched or dropped or mailed or sprouted. In this way your child is no different from any other.

• *Depersonalize whenever possible.* Make the birth parents' decision not about your child but about any baby born at that time. Try something like, "Amanda wasn't able to take care of a new baby, no matter who that would be, at the time you were born."

• *Answer only what is asked.* If your daughter asks where she came from, that doesn't have to lead to a discussion about sex. The answer could be as simple as "You were born, just like all babies are, when Amanda gave birth to you." (You might notice that the middle phrase in this sentence, *just like all babies are*, reinforces that your daughter is no different from other people.)

• *Similarly, make sure you understand what is being asked.* If you son asks, "Where did I come from?" he may be asking in what city was he born, whether he was born in a hospital or in a car on the side of the road, who gave birth to him, or a host of other possibilities based on whatever framework he's operating under at the time (my son asked this question after a family friend gave birth in a Volkswagen Bug). It's wise to ask for clarification about what your child is actually asking before proceeding with an answer. "Do you mean what city were you born in?" or "Are you asking me which hospital you were born in?" or "Tell me what you're wanting to know." Clarify, clarify, clarify before charting a course of conversation.

- *Not all questions will lead to sex (but many will).* Just as when you tell an adoption story, the more comfortable you can be with the answers around a sex question, the more smoothly your conversation will unfold. If you feel embarrassment or dread, you will be more likely to stumble and your child may feel less comfortable asking you the next time he has a Deep Question.

  And with sex discussions, just as with adoption stories, if you have a series of little talks you never have to have The Big Talk.

- *Birth-father questions are more likely to lead to a sex talk.* It's one thing to explain a birth mother to a child. It's concrete—the child sees a pregnant woman, you explain that there's a baby in there and that soon the baby will be born (you can get as descriptive as you and your child are ready to). You explain that every baby grows in a mother's body.

  But the concept of a birth father is harder for a child to grasp. *He didn't get a big belly. He didn't carry me around. He may not have even been there when I was born. So just what is this guy's connection to me?*

  If discussions about a birth father lead you into facts-of-life territory, I suggest following the KISS principle—Keep It Simple, Sweetheart. "A baby is made when an egg from a woman and a sperm from a man meet and form a new person." If pressed (and only if pressed) you could also say, "The egg and sperm can meet in a woman's body after the man and the woman have sex." (Children conceived by gamete donation also face some of the same issues that adopted children do, so your sentence here might be, "An egg from me and a sperm from a man whom I selected to be your father met in my body/at the doctor's office, and you were created.") Let your child lead you by allowing him to either ask more questions or indicate he's had his fill of the topic for now. Tune in so that you can tell which he needs.

- *Examine your own hesitations* if you find it difficult to have these talks with your child. Resolve any of your own problems about residual infertility grief, insecurity about not being the only mother or father, or jealousy about the role another holds in her life. Do not allow your issues to become your child's.

Over the years, as my children cognitively grow, they sense the layers and nuance of their stories. We strive to make our home an open environment where our children are free to wonder aloud and give voice to their innermost thoughts. Our role is not to "fix" any feelings of loss that arise or to smooth everything over for them. Rather, it's to give our children the space to feel all their feelings, without judgment and with open hearts, and to support them as they work through their emotions, trusting in the process and teaching them to do so, as well.

TESSA MEETS JOE

Not all open adoptions include both the birth mother and the birth father from the beginning. In these cases, a search-and-reunion leg of the tour may be in order. Earlier in this chapter I told you how Tessa began her reunion with her birth father, Joe, and the push-pull she felt that caused her great turmoil. Here is the rest of that story.

Finally, the day of the "reunion" arrived (actually, there was no "re" about it, as they had never met previously). As my husband, two children, and I approached the restaurant where we were to meet Joe, we could see through the window that he and his family had already arrived. Roger and Reed walked in, and I followed, carrying Tessa. My seven-year-old was glued to my hip, her head buried in my neck, not yet ready to see or be seen.

Roger and Joe greeted each other and introduced the children. Reed and Joe's son immediately started wielding imaginary swords. Joe's wife, Amy, tended to one-year-old Ivy. When we all sat down to chat, Tessa rearranged herself to stay hidden in my lap.

After five minutes of small talk, suddenly the Tessa Show began. In a flash, she was hugging Joe. She spent the rest of dinner on his lap, talking and laughing. Joe was happy to oblige. When it was time to head home, we said our goodbyes. At that point, Tessa had to be pried off Joe.

Over the next few months, we saw each other regularly. Roger and I felt good about the "reunion." Until a few months later when Tessa experienced some more turmoil.

By that time, one-on-one visits with Crystal had become commonplace. These visits had worked well for all of us, so it seemed okay to say yes to Joe when he asked to spend an afternoon with Tessa. When I bounced the idea off her, she squealed with delight. Roger and I asked ourselves all the safety questions and felt confident that Tessa would be in good hands with Joe and Amy.

So we set the afternoon up. We met Joe for the exchange, planning to retrieve Tessa several hours later. Beforehand I'd talked with my daughter about expectations (we always do this when approaching a social event) and had told her I would call to check on her often. We'd even come up with a code word for her to use in case she wanted me to come get her early.

When I did call, via Joe's cell phone, each time she said she was having a *great time*!

At the end of the afternoon, our two families met for an early dinner. I could see that Tessa and Ivy had bonded and that Tessa was glowing. Well done, I thought.

But two weeks later, at bedtime, Tessa freaked out. "I don't want to have four parents! Mom, take away all these pictures of Crystal and Joe!" She climbed up to her shelf and threw unframed photos at me. "Mom, call them both tomorrow, and tell them I never want to see them again!"

The next day, while Tessa was at school, I called Joe with the news, breaking his heart. In a brave voice he said he was happy to have had the time he did.

When I picked up Tessa from school, she asked if I had called her birth parents. I told her I had reached Joe, but not Crystal. Tessa replied, "I changed my mind. I think I can still see Crystal." She didn't want to discuss it any further, and I couldn't imagine what had happened to cause this dramatic about-face.

For a long time afterward, I feared that I had messed everything up by embracing open adoption so wholeheartedly. Had I been too enthusiastic about keeping Crystal in our lives? Too insistent on bringing Joe in?

I gained some insight from a wise counselor who helped me figure out that for Tessa it wasn't that the previous seven years of openness had been a mistake, but that the episode with Joe had been, simply, too much, too soon.

Tessa is a child who needs boundaries. She must, at all times, know how far she can go with a given person in a given situation. She is constantly testing my boundaries as well as others'. It's her way of figuring out her world and feeling secure in it.

And although she was eager to spend that afternoon with Joe, she couldn't have known the feelings that would result. Not because Joe was unsupportive, but because having him in her life was different and unfamiliar. And maybe she even started contemplating her Road Not Taken. Profound implications come with that thought.

In time, Tessa processed this episode, and soon she resumed telephone contact with Joe. She eventually did ask to see him again, but not without Roger and me as her tethers. Eventually Tessa met Joe's mom and stepfather, as well as a brother or two of Joe's. I was relieved that she'd ultimately been able to incorporate this branch of important people onto her family tree.

In looking back over this episode I've learned that upheavals may happen and when they do it doesn't necessarily mean we've done something wrong. In fact, the processing behind the upheavals can be a *good* thing, in that enduring a small emotional tremor now is better than unleashing twenty or thirty years of pent-up energy in one massive breakdown.

> I also notice that keeping my own heart open—to Tessa's thoughts, to my own intuition and guidance, to Joe—and trusting in the process of open-hearted parenting are key to helping Tessa fully integrate herself.

BRANCHING OUT

We've explored maintaining openness with your child during private conversations about adoption (and possibly about sex); now let's devote some time to openness with not just the birth mother but the whole birth family.

Building your family via adoption may very well mean welcoming more than just one person to your mix. Likely you add your child's first mother. Possibly you add your child's first father. But developing a relationship with a child's first parents is just the tip of what may be a very large iceberg. There may also be biological grandparents, aunts, uncles, cousins, siblings. And half-siblings and stepsiblings. Clearly, the better parents are at navigating these relationships, the easier time the child will have in integrating all the pieces of his or her biology.

Adoptive mom Luna, whom we met at the very beginning of her open adoption in chapter 1, has this to say about embracing first-family members for her daughter, Jaye:

As the first grandchild (and great-grandchild), our daughter holds a special place in her birth-family lineage. The main reason we felt it was important to establish such connection is simply because *these people became our family*, too. There are no good words to describe these relationships, yet they are now extended family.

When we first met our future child's family, we wanted to get to know them, to build a foundation for a future relationship. Kaye's mom shared Kaye's baby book so we could see what she was like as a little girl. Kaye's grandmother shared stories about Kaye's mom and aunts and about her awe at becoming a great-grandmother. Kaye's dad shared important family history and stories. Kaye's little brother shared his excitement about being an uncle. Naturally, it was important for them to see and enjoy their first (great-) grandchild and only niece. They had waited a long time to meet her too. In the early days of our open adoption, it was tremendously affirming to be treated as our baby's parents by her family of origin. Not only did we learn vital information about our daughter's background to share with her one day, we were embraced as her parents and we established important relationships for a lifetime.

Now we share important milestones and silly anecdotes. We celebrate birthdays and certain holidays together. At nearly three years old, Jaye is not yet old enough to understand her adoption story, yet no doubt she appreciates these significant people in her life. She simply recognizes them as family. Jaye wants to hear about every photograph we have of her with them, and already I can see how these connections will help her process her story some day. For now, Jaye has every right to feel their love and care, to experience their affection firsthand. It's true that *you can never have too many people to love a child.* Her maternal grandmother often notes the benefits of openness for them too. Every time we visit she says how wonderful it is to share Jaye's life with us. Now we all marvel at this amazing little girl as she grows.

Some day our daughter may have a relationship with her birth family distinct from ours. We can't know what the future holds, but maintaining these important relationships can help provide Jaye a critical connection later.

We also have a relationship—though to a much lesser extent—with Jaye's birth father's family. We met her birth grandmother twice, and we keep in touch through e-mail and photos. Because we don't have much contact with her biological father, it's important for us to try and maintain some connection there. Not only is [Jaye's biological paternal grandmother] interested in her first grandchild, but this relationship may be all that Jaye has on that side. It's important to keep an open door to her heritage.[4]

When asked about welcoming her daughter's extended birth family, mom Angie says, "Why do we do it, have contact with our son's birth parents, birth sister, and birth grandparents? I guess I would counter with *why not?* In the long run, our son will know more about his birth family and already have those relationships where he can approach them to ask those inevitable questions that will come up as he gets older."[5]

THE DREADED WORD *REAL*: WHAT DOES *REAL FAMILY* MEAN?

It will come up. Your child will, at least once, if not more, explore the word *real* as it pertains to his identity and his family. It happened the first time in an unexpected way for me.

We were happy to hear that my son's birth mom had put us on her itinerary during her visit to Colorado the summer that Reed was seven. Reed hadn't had contact with her in nearly four years, and for the first time he was to meet his half-siblings, ages three and one.

Reed showed no signs of either distress or euphoria in the weeks leading up to Michele's visit or during her dinner with us. Nor after she left. For him and for her, Even Keel seemed to be the name of the game.

The surprise was in a conversation with Reed's sister, Tessa. "You know, Mom," she said one night, "Reed's not my *real* brother. He's just a step."

My heart stopped and then broke into pieces. Since the first day of adoption school nearly ten years before, I had been prepared to be discounted as a real mom, but it had never occurred to me that my children might discount each other. I was saddened and knocked off balance, not knowing what to say.

So I resorted to my habits when I get adoption stress: Breathe. Be aware of my breathing. Silently ask for wisdom and guidance.

"What does it mean, Tessa, to be a real brother or sister?" I probed.

"It means you have the same parents. Reed and I don't have the same parents, so we're just steps."

"You mean because your birth parents are Joe and Crystal and Reed's are Michele and AJ?"

"Yeah. We come from different parents. So we're just steps," she repeated the phrase that she was stuck on, that we were now both stuck on.

Tessa had been trying to figure out "steps" since reuniting with Joe two years before. Joe and his wife have a daughter (Tessa's younger half-sister), and the wife has a son from a previous marriage, Joe's stepson. Who was, in explicit terms, her birth stepbrother (or step-birth-brother?).

Likewise, Crystal has a son (Tessa's older half-brother), and Crystal's then-boyfriend also had a son, who was not technically Crystal's stepson but was considered a full-fledged son. This boy was, explicitly, Tessa's practically birth stepbrother.

Got all that? It's a lot for anyone, especially for the nine year old in the center of it. If only *step* were as straightforward as the stool Tessa was perched on.

"Well, Sweetie," I began, "could it be that you and Reed actually have *two* sets of *real* parents?" I emphasized the words that encompassed and validated.

"No, Mommmmm," she said, exasperated with me, feeling prickly. "*Real* means the people who are really your parents, the ones who made you."

So I pulled out my stock answer, which I'd thought would be used only on curious strangers unacquainted with Positive Adoption Language. And I spontaneously added some levity.

"Well, you know what *that* means, don't you?" I said with a twinkle in my eye.

"What?" Tessa said uneasily, realizing I was about to get her.

"That means . . ." I picked her up (I could still do that, though not for much longer) ". . . that means that Fake Mom changed five thousand of your diapers!" I tickled her sides.

"And Fake Mom sang you all those lullabies!" I tickled her underpits (as Reed calls them). I got nose-to-nose with her, giggled hysterically with her, locked eyes with her.

She joined the game. "Fake Mom makes me do my homework! Fake Mom tickles me! Fake Mom takes me for pedicures!"

Soon we were out of breath from laughing so hard.

I propped myself up on my elbow and brought the level down a bit. "Sweetie, both Crystal and I are real. Both Joe and Daddy are real. And Reed is real, too. Who fights with you over popsicle flavors? Not Fake Brother. Who annoys you when you have a friend over? Who plays School with you and always lets you be the teacher? No Fake People live in this house."

"I know what you mean, Mama." I know she calls me *Mama* when she has softened. Just then, Michele, who had been playing with Reed and his birth siblings in the backyard, walked in. Tessa and I pulled ourselves up and joined her. The conversation was over. This time.

I realize that there was no final resolution, no definitive happy ending, to this very complex issue that day. Rather, we're living a mere pause in what will be a very long story arc. But there had been progress in our process. Tessa and I had worked through something, we connected, we allowed each other space to explore and talk. We stayed real.

BACK TO THE FUTURE

Before we move on let's do an exercise. I'm giving you an assignment, one that requires you to project your open-adoption parenting intentions and efforts from the present time into some future time. This is the same exercise tackled by a group of open-adoption bloggers at a 2010 Open Adoption Roundtable. Here we go.

Imagine your child as an adult describing their open-adoption experience. What do you hope they will be able to say about you? How did you view their other parents? In what ways did you support their relationship with them?[6]

This exercise asks you to consider a time when the hard work is behind you and you are able to see clearly what you have helped nourish and tend. It asks you to get into the head of this grown-up child and write a letter to you, the parent, about how you handled all this adoption stuff.

Now go write that letter.

FROM HUNKY-DORY TO STORMY

This chapter has walked us down the sunny side of the street—we've traveled easy paths that wind gently, and we've observed adventures that eventually end well. But what about the shady side? What do we do when things just don't work out the way we want them to? Let's talk about the tough stuff in the next chapter.

7

REALITY CHECK: WHEN IT'S NOT EASY

Some would have you believe that adoption is all love and rainbows and unicorns.[1] *Everybody wins! The birth parents will move on without a hitch! The adoptive parents will parent their child without a hitch! The child will grow up without a hitch!* Clearly, this is not fully true—there will be hitches. Not because of adoption necessarily, but because of *life*.

Others would have you believe that adoption is rooted in loss. The adoptive parents lose the dream of having a biological child. The birthparents lose a child. And the child loses parents.

I do not question the veracity of this claim but rather the wisdom in claiming it. Adoption can just as easily be viewed as problem *solving*: people who long to parent get to; people who are unable to parent at a certain time have a way to opt out; a child gets parents who are eager and able to be there, wholeheartedly and forever.

Adoption apologists are apt to create adoption *victims*. On the other hand open-hearted open adoption *empowers* those involved—the opposite of victimhood. It empowers the adoptive parents to be secure in their role as life sustainers. It empowers birth parents to be involved at an equally important level as life givers. And it empowers the adopted person to become full of himself, the parts that come from *both* sets of his parents.

Nevertheless, it is possible—even probable—that an open-adoption constellation will, at times, experience difficulties and that an adopted person will, at times, struggle in processing and integrating his adoptedness. In this chapter we explore some of the common bumps in the road experienced specifically by adoptive parents and their adopted kids and examine how many families have dealt with them. We devote all of chapter 9 to birth parents, exploring hitches they commonly experience on this journey.

But first we begin this chapter with an overview of core issues in adoption and how they relate to a child's cognitive and emotional growth. We'll look at some common hitches that can arise. And, finally, adult adoptees share what their parents did and said that helped—and what didn't.

PSYCHOSOCIAL STAGES AND CORE ADOPTION ISSUES

Erik Erikson was a twentieth-century psychoanalyst known for coining the term *identity crisis*. Erikson's paternal parentage was unknown to him, and *Wikipedia* says that "the development of identity seems to have been one of Erikson's greatest concerns in his own life as well as in his theory. During his childhood and early adulthood he was known as Erik Homberger, and his parents kept the details of his birth a secret."[2]

According to Erikson, every person progresses through a series of eight life stages. The five reached before adulthood are what concern us here. Note that the exact age at which each stage is reached may be affected by biological, emotional, and social factors.

1. *Trust versus mistrust (birth to eighteen months).* A child develops a sense of trust when his needs are met—sustenance, safety, stability, and affection. A lack in these areas leads to mistrust.
2. *Autonomy versus shame (eighteen to thirty-six months).* A child gains a measure of self-control and independence when learning physical skills, such as walking and potty training. Failure to begin to control himself results in shame.
3. *Initiative versus guilt (three to six years).* A child develops personal power by controlling his environment and making things happen. Too much or too little personal power induces guilt.
4. *Industry versus inferiority (six to twelve years).* A child navigates social and academic spheres. Success results in a sense of industry; lack of success prompts a sense of inferiority.

5. *Identity versus role confusion (twelve years through the teen years)*. A teenager develops a sense of personal identity in his various social groups. Success enables him to remain true to himself (because the self is well-defined), and lack leads to confusion and a weak sense of self.[3]

For adopted kids, things tend to be even more complex. In addition to Erickson's life stages, parents should also be aware of adoption's core issues, as defined by Deborah N. Silverstein and Sharon Roszia:

- *Loss.* The child has trouble holding on and letting go.
- *Rejection.* He suffers a fear of abandonment, feelings of not being good enough to stay with.
- *Guilt and shame.* He believes that he doesn't deserve good fortune and struggles with anger.
- *Grief.* Unresolved childhood grief can lead to him to depression or anger.
- *Identity.* He grapples with integrating all the pieces of himself, asking, *Who am I, and where did I come from?*
- *Intimacy and relationships.* He may bond inappropriately—too soon, too late, too intensely, not at all—because he fears risk, loss, rejection, and abandonment.
- *Control.* Realizing that adoption was done to him, he experiences a sense of powerlessness, of being at the mercy of fate.[4]

These core issues can be at play for an adopted child during any of Erikson's stages. While growing up is tricky for anybody, issues inherent in adoption bring additional layers of identity formation to navigate. Parents of adopted children must realize that the road may have a few extra bumps and might be a little more interesting. Simply by knowing that these core issues exist, parents can choose to react appropriately (not deny them and not dwell on them) when they arise in their adopted children.

We support our children by allowing them to feel their feelings and *move through them*. In enabling movement—keeping emotions in motion—our children are less likely to get stuck in a stage or on an issue. And with openness in adoption the child can work out his identity and self-worth in the open, with the assistance of his parents and possibly birth-family members, not alone under a cloud of secrecy.

HITCHES FOR ADOPTIVE PARENTS

Every member of the adoption constellation—birth parent, adoptive parent, and child—contends with issues unique to their role. Advanced awareness of what struggles can look like empowers us to most effectively cope with them when they arise, so we're going to spend a good deal of time carefully identifying and considering them.[5]

Let's start with the adoptive parents, whose challenges are often mentally formulated as "Buts."

But We're Afraid They'll Change Their Minds

Adoptive parents are vulnerable to this fear from the time of a match until the time of relinquishment. The time span is usually of short duration—cold comfort for such intensity.

We said in chapter 2 that the birth parents' decision to place must be made all over again after the baby is born. The question hopeful adopting parents must answer is how open and vulnerable they should make themselves during the waiting time. A defense mechanism keeps out the bad and the good equally, so guarding the heart should be done consciously and judiciously. Just how open can you afford to be?

Roger and I chose the cautiously optimistic path when waiting for Crystal to give birth to her baby and recommit to placing him or her. We would not believe it was real until it was real; we remained positive but did not indulge in exuberance. This stance cast a pall on our demeanor, one that Crystal noticed. It was she who helped us lighten up in the days leading to Tessa's birth and placement. One of the things Crystal wanted from her prebirth match was for us to be happy. We were fearful of being happy—and of showing happiness.

CRYSTAL SAYS: I didn't see myself as a sinner, and I didn't feel I needed salvation by placing my baby with someone more deserving, but I did want good things to come from my decision to place, other than my baby having a life I couldn't provide at the time. I wanted to do everything I could to get this baby started off on the right track. And that right track involved being born into joy.

I could see that Roger and Lori were hesitant to get too happy about the upcoming birth. They were spooked about getting baby clothes and even a car seat. But I wanted them to be happy. *Their being happy was going to be good for my baby.* I realized I needed to give them permission to feel their joy.

So I told them that being happy was not only okay with me, I expected it! Lori said that she was worried about being happy and *showing* me that she was happy because her happiness was tied in with my sadness. I told her that I was going to be sad no matter how happy they were or weren't, and that I knew her joy wasn't about my sadness but about the joy of this new baby who was about to be born, a baby who deserved to be greeted in this world with happiness. Happiness about him or her.

Things lightened up after that conversation. Roger and Lori were cautiously giddy from that point on, and seeing their happiness actually made things easier for me.

Something else to keep in mind: if the decision to place is the right one for the placing parents, it will be right no matter how much time they spend with their newborn. One hopeful mother, Meg—whom we first met in chapter 4—was alarmed when the expectant mom she was matched with wanted to bring the baby home for some of her state's seventy-two-hour waiting period between birth and relinquishment. The expectant mom asked Meg what she thought about that request.

What could Meg say? She was confused and fearful. How could she be honest about her feelings yet avoid making the relationship adversarial?

Adoption social workers tell us that for a mother to say good-bye to her baby, she must first say hello. Time in the hospital, for this reason, is very helpful for both the placing mother (and father) and the baby. For a hopeful mom like Meg, though, it can be anxiety inducing. *Will everything proceed as planned, or will the other parents find it unthinkable and undoable to say good-bye to that baby, just as I do?*

Meg and her husband stayed open to the possibility of the adoption and also took steps to try to disconnect from the outcome (which, as you can imagine, is very difficult). As Meg shared in chapter 4, the adoption did not go through, but it wasn't because of anything Meg and her husband did or didn't do, did well or did poorly. It's hard to be in a powerless position, and the best we can do at such times is to remain open and present, trusting that we'll have the resources we need to deal with the hand we are dealt. Staying open may make potential pain a little more intense, but closing up can make relationships and situations more rigid and less workable. It's a balancing act of risk and reward, and each person must figure out what his or her personal balance is.

Months after the loss of her dream, Meg's reflected on the scenario. "In interactions with the expectant mom, I think we did need to be positive and act as though it was going to happen. But when away from her I wish I'd modulated my emotions. I still would have felt grief, but it would have been easier on me had I not been so certain, so invested in the outcome we wanted."[6]

But I Feel the Birth Mother's Pain Too Acutely; I Feel Guilty

Because of the gratitude that an adopting parent feels toward a placing parent, there can be transference of other emotions, like grief or guilt. It is important that through mindfulness we remain empathetic for those involved in our open adoption but do not take on feelings that don't belong to us, especially burdensome ones. Doing so does not serve anyone—not the adoptive parent, not the birth parent, and especially not the child. If this is an issue you struggle with, begin to recognize when you are taking on another person's feelings and, with that awareness, simply decide not to. *This does not mean you lack compassion*; it's simply a way of establishing healthy boundaries within yourself.

Awareness is the key. If you are aware of your feelings, you can make a conscious decision whether to accept a feeling or not. It's using reason with emotion, and it's with awareness that we can effect change.

But the Birth Parents Don't Respect Our Boundaries

You can't change the other person; you can change only your own thoughts, beliefs, and actions. Examine your own role in the situation, and do a quick check: Are you setting clear boundaries? Are they reasonable boundaries? Do any of your boundaries result from your own fears and insecurities? If you were in the other position of the relationship, how would the boundary issue look to you? A good way to check for reasonableness and clarity is to use the in-law test from chapter 3: if this were an in-law instead of a birth parent, how would you set and enforce your boundaries? If you have difficulty setting and defending boundaries, consider taking an assertiveness class to find a middle stance between aggression and passive-aggression, which will help you do what you can do and accept the rest.

But the Birth Parents Have Pulled Away

Adoptions do sometimes close, but it's not always the adoptive parents closing them. Sometimes it's a first parent who takes a step back. Again, there are limits to what an adoptive parent can do when this happens. Do a self-check: Have you been open and inviting? Have you been sensitive and empathetic to the first parents' perspectives? Are you keeping your child at the center of your decisions about and demeanor toward his birth parents?

If your self-examination reveals that you need to make amends for something you did or didn't do or for the spirit in which you related, try to remedy the situation as you would with any other extended family member.

You may very well plumb your depths and find there's nothing you did that caused the pulling away and nothing you can do to reverse it. The best you can do is keep contact information for your child's first parent in order to maintain a thread of contact and periodically check in, always pleasantly. *Hey, just wanted to let you know that Jimmy starts kindergarten next week! As always, we include you in our nighttime prayers. Hope to hear from you when you can.* Or, *It would mean the world to Jimmy if you would call him next week for his birthday. We'd both love to hear your voice.*

You may also want to write a note to your child's birth parents, sharing with them why you want to keep them in your lives. In chapter 9 you'll find a template that you can change to fit your circumstances and your voice.

With this hitch, like with the others, you fix what you can and accept what you can't. Much of our approach to building open-adoption relationships is reminiscent of the spirit of the "Serenity Prayer" by Reinhold Niebuhr, often associated with twelve-step programs:

Give us courage to change what must be altered
Serenity to accept what cannot be helped
And the insight to know the one from the other.[7]

HITCHES FOR ADOPTEES

We adoptive parents continually walk a fine line: we don't want to *dwell* on adoption and assign every growing-up difficulty to it, yet we also don't want to *deny* its effects and not see, hear, or know when something adoption-related is going on. To walk this line requires us to cultivate mindfulness, clarity, and inner calm, to tune in to ourselves and our child—especially during moments of stress—and be responsive rather than reactive.

"Am I a Bastard?"

In addition to the word *real* defining a familial relationship, another dreaded word for adoptive parents is *bastard*. For me it came up when Tessa, then ten, asked what *bitch* meant and if it were a bad word. We'd had this talk before, so I told her again that the dictionary meaning is *a female dog* but that some people have also made it into a hurtful word meant to show extreme disrespect. If the word is used as a weapon, then, yes, it is a bad word.

I was ready for all that. But not for the next part.

"Mommy, what does *bastard* mean? Is it a bad word, too?"

Bitch was easy—though its connotation is an insult, its denotation is neutral. But *bastard* is different. Its dictionary meaning is, itself, a highly charged slur against "a person born of unmarried parents."[8] My instinct, unfortunately, was to go straight to the dictionary meaning, to which Tessa replied, "That means I'm a bastard, right?"

Though it was clear that Tessa bestowed the word with no negative meaning (she said it matter-of-factly, just trying to put pieces together) I, myself, felt a shock at the declaration and was unprepared for my reaction and struggled how to proceed.

Because I didn't, in that moment, have a response I thought was good enough, I gave myself permission to table the discussion (you know you can do that, right?) until I could examine the issue and see where different approaches would take us. I took to the Internet and asked others involved in adoption for insight and input. They were generous and astute, and two days later I was ready to get back to The Bastard Talk, armed with these points:

- Find out the context in which she heard the word.
- Answer only what she asks, and make sure I understand exactly what she's asking.
- Reinforce that what's acceptable socially has changed from the "old days."
- Keep it real so that Tessa is prepared to navigate the world she lives in. And don't skirt the issue—my discomfort would give the word added power.
- Ask questions to check for her understanding.
- Dissolve shame by pointing out how ridiculous it is to put such a word on a baby or a child.

I then had to find a good time and a good entry point. Play and movement are effective backdrops, and when an opportunity arose I seized it.

Tessa was breathless, taking a break after dancing in our living room for the umpteenth time to Journey's "Don't Stop Believing." I'd been masquerading as the entire audience at Radio City Music Hall.

"Tessa, do you remember the other day when you asked about the word *bastard*?"

"Yeah . . ."

"I'm wondering how you heard it used" (said with as much openness as I could muster).

"A sixth-grade boy yelled it at a guy who stole a basketball from him."

"Oh. So what do you think he meant by that?"

"That he was being mean."

"Yeah, that he was being a jerk, right? That's usually what people mean when they use that word. It's kind of like the male version of *bitch*. And you know that both words are meant to hurt and are very disrespectful and very inappropriate."

Dramatic: "I know that, Mommmmmmm."

"And you also know that *bastard* can mean someone who was born to parents who weren't married, right?"

"Yeah, like Crystal and Joe weren't married when I was born."

"That's true . . . You know, I always thought it was crazy to have that word be about a kid—even a baby—when the baby really didn't do anything except be born."

"Mom. It's not like they're saying the baby is a jerk."

"Of course not. No baby is a jerk. But in the olden days when unmarried people were not allowed to live together, it was a rude word that described a child born to them."

"That's so not fair to the baby!"

"Exactly. Sometimes a word says more about the person who uses it than about the person it's aimed at."

"I know, Mom. You're telling me not to call people names, right?"

"You're so smart. Hey, another thing. The other day you wondered if you were a bastard. What do you think?"

"Wellll . . . I kinda am because of Crystal and Joe. But I'm kinda not because of you and Dad." (pause) "But I definitely am not a jerk."

"Most of the time." (smiling)

"Mo-o-o-ommmm." (smiling back)

"These days, we don't talk bad about children for anything that's really about their parents. So, no, I cannot think of any way that anyone would consider you a bastard."

"Okay. Mom. Wanna watch me dance again?"

Confusion

Some people assume that open adoption will confuse the child. *How will the child know who her real parents are? Surely it's too hard for her to figure out everybody's roles. Four parents? Too many! Too much!*

Jim Gritter, a social worker with decades of experience dealing with adoptions issues, responds to this line of thinking by asking in return, "Is it your experience that when you're well-informed, you're confused?"[9]

One could make the case that it's closedness in adoption, not openness, that contributes to confusion. Sara, an adult adoptee, shares this conundrum commonly experienced by adopted people:

I did feel confused (and to some extent still am) as to whether I could claim my adopted-family lineage as my own, given that our relationship was not genetic but merely legal. But in reverse I am also unsettled because while I share a genetic lineage with my biological family I am unable, by law, to claim any relation to that group. What this has resulted in is a lifetime of never feeling that I fit into a family completely, even though I look like my biological family and share childhood memories with my adopted family.[10]

In an open adoption it's the adults who are more likely to suffer confusion. For example, sometimes my children will call their respective birth moms simply Mom. *Mom, what state does my mom live in?* Or the birth dad simply Dad or even Daddy. *Let's call my daddy after the game and tell him how I did!*

Is Tessa confused? Is Reed? Do these words show that they don't know the roles we adults play in their lives?

I think my children know precisely who contributes what. But me? The first few times I heard this I wanted to jump in and correct my children. *You mean your birth mom?* Or *Daddy's your daddy. AJ is your birth dad.* But I stopped myself from reacting without first dropping into self-awareness. The terms did, at first, bug me because I felt they diminished the roles Roger and I play as our children's everyday parents.

With reflection I realized that allowing my children to use whatever words they wanted did two things: First, it lets me know what my children are really thinking, not what they *think* I want them to think. If I could get past this rather small irritation, my children would continue giving me access to their private thoughts, confident they could trust me not to judge or censor them. Second, it shows to what degree my children are incorporating the biological pieces of themselves. If, suddenly, a less-endearing term were used, it could be a clue that Tessa or Reed were processing a birth-parent relationship and that I should tune in more deeply to see if my assistance were needed.

Intimacy

Intimacy means allowing someone to see the true you, warts and all. It happens when you are aware and authentic and able to make yourself vulnerable, when you are comfortable enough with your Self that your own opinion of you trumps anyone else's. It is hindered when you relate from fear or insecurity, because then you try to hide, avoid, or put off.

Intimacy is also hindered, in the case of having adoption talks, when you borrow words from others that may or may not fit. Rebecca Hawkes, who blogs at Love Is Not a Pie, is a mom in an open adoption as well as an adoptee. She tells us how fear of not knowing their own right words prevented her parents from relating with her at a deeper level of intimacy.

> In my teens I found a pamphlet in my baby book called "How to Talk to Your Adopted Child about Adoption," and in it *all the words my parents had spoken to me over the years on the subject.* I understood two things in that moment: one was that my parents had educated themselves and tried to do their best by me, according the information available at the time; the second was that they had been working from a script and had never had a real, honest, from-the-heart discussion with me about my adoption.
>
> That conversation happened a few years down the line. I was sitting with my adoptive mom in a pizza parlor, and we had recently learned that my brother's girlfriend, a high-school senior, was pregnant. A conversation about that situation led to our first-ever frank discussion about my history, including the revelation that my mom knew more than I had previously realized about the identity of my biological mother. Later that afternoon she placed a newspaper clipping in my hand, and for the first time in my life I saw a photo of a face that looked like mine. [11]

Rebecca's belated discussion with her mom helped her begin to make some important connections between her genetic makeup and her cultural makeup. Such a moment of intimacy might have happened earlier in Rebecca's life had her mother felt empowered to speak from her heart rather than through a book. Meaningful revelations like Rebecca's are why in this book we encourage you to develop a mind-set, a heart-set, from which you can tap into your own inner wisdom and through self-awareness be authentic and intimate with your child.

Dealing with the Road Not Taken

Some may think that a child being able to see his road not taken will cause unnecessary eruptions and that not knowing would be better for him. Openness is not the *cause* of any eruptions but instead can actually be part of the *solution* to them. If you've established an open relation-ship with your child, he is more likely to allow you into his innermost thoughts and fears. He then doesn't have to face them without you. But if you are closed, he is more alone.

The adoption road is multiforked, with countless paths not taken. Adoptive parents have them—*What if we had tried fertility treatments again? What if the birth parents had picked someone else? What if the birth mom had chosen a different agency? What if we hadn't ended up with this child?* Our what-ifs are endless. And our children have them, as well.

In lower elementary school, my children began to understand that they, too, have paths not taken. Tessa had seen both Crystal and Joe parenting (separately) her half-siblings. She'd been to their homes. She had wondered aloud, on occasion, what it would be like to live with Joe or Crystal. Would she have a dog? Would she have her own room? Would she have fewer chores, a later bedtime, more Dr Pepper? What would it feel like to see her own face in those of the people raising her?

Reed had not vocalized his thoughts about living with either or both of his birth parents. But he did ask his big what-if question: *What if someone else had become his parents?* While his sister saw the singular possibility of her biological parents raising her, Reed understood that he could have ended up with, well, just about anyone.

The late Betty Jean Lifton, PhD, herself an adoptee in a closed adoption and an advocate for open adoptions, called this phenomenon our "ghosts," which she theorized can haunt members of an adoption triad.

- *Adoptee.* On one side of the adoptee is the ghost of the child he might have been had he stayed with his birth mother. On the other side is the ghost of the child his parents might have had, or the child who died; this ghost is like a sibling rival, who the adoptee may try to compete with, or give up on without even trying. And there is the ghost of the birth mother, from whom the adoptee has never fully disconnected, the ghost of the birth father, and the birth clan.
- *Birth mother.* As we'll explore in chapter 9, the birth mother is accompanied by the ghost of the baby she gave up, the ghost of

the mother she might have been, and the ghost of the adoptive parents who are raising her child.

- *Adoptive parents.* The adoptive parents are shadowed by the ghost of the perfect child they might have had and by the ghost of the birth mother and birth father, whose child they are raising.[12]

Not all ghosts may apply in your situation, but the concept can help us help our children process their ghosts, their roads not taken. How? Openness helps by simply acknowledging the fact that the wondering may happen from time to time *and that it's okay.* Openness can help remove the mystery about birth parents that used to be resolved only through search and reunion. To assist your child in exploring the road not taken and ultimately embracing the one that *was* taken, first come to peace with your own roads not taken, and, second, keep your heart open so that communication with your child can remain unobstructed. Give him the space to feel his feelings and share his wonderings on the outside of himself. Dissolve your own triggers and snags so that you can focus only on his.

Simple. Not necessarily easy.

Trust

All humans deal with developing varying degrees of trust, as Erikson posited; it's not a stage unique to an adopted person. But adoption does add another facet to building and maintaining a trusting relationship. Andy, an adoptive mom in Canada, is herself, an adoptee who blogs about her dual role in the adoption triad at *Today's the Day They Give Babies Away*. About how she was parented in the 1970s, she says:

> My parents mostly did all the right things. They told me at a very young age that I was adopted; it was never a secret. One thing I wish they had done differently occurred when my mom applied for and received a packet of nonidentifying information about my first family. She got this information when I was thirteen after I asked her to get it, as I was underage and could not apply myself. The information arrived within six months. Want to know when my mother gave it to me? Seventeen years later when I was thirty!
>
> Her reason for not giving it to me sooner? I stopped asking for it. At thirteen, six months is a long time to wait. I asked a few times

during the first weeks but then stopped asking—not because I no longer wanted it, but because I *trusted my mom* to tell me when it arrived. Even I was surprised by the betrayal I felt when I found out that she had been sitting on this information that was so precious to me for so long without bothering to tell me that she had it.[13]

Mapping and Avoiding the Parents' Minefields

Andy was attuned to her mother's emotions, especially those surrounding adoption. "I thought about adoption a lot, but I didn't really talk about it much. While my parents were open and honest with me, I knew that it also caused my mother some grief to talk about it. In hindsight, I know that she must have had a lot of unresolved grief around her fertility issues (she had several miscarriages after adopting me). But as a child I thought the grief was because of me, so I didn't bring it up."[14]

Sometimes the mapping is done accurately and sometimes not. A child is the center of her universe, and there are stages in which it is normal for her to think that everything big has to do with her. When Andy perceived her mother grieving about children, she naturally assumed the grief was about her in some way. Her mother didn't know about this assumption and could not, therefore, clarify it. Andy figured out early on that her mother had a grief trigger and that it quite possibly was Andy herself—a big burden for a little girl to carry.

What does it look like to be a triggerless parent? Because I'm someone who flips her lid about dirty underpants left in the hallway and bike helmets not worn religiously, I can't tell you. But I can share this story about remaining triggerless in an adoption processing moment with my son when he was eight years old.

Just before bedtime one night, Reed and I read entries from his new *Guinness Book of World Records* and marveled at crazy human feats. We put the book down to cuddle, just the two of us, in my bed.

"Do you think often about Michele?" I opened the door to talk about his birth mom, as I occasionally do.

"Yeah. A lot . . . Mom, do you think I could try living with her for a week or a month or something?"

"Sweetie," I replied, "it doesn't work like that. But we can certainly try to arrange for a visit with Michele the next time we are all in the same state."

"Okay, Mama," Reed said. A moment later: "Mom, why did Michele give me away? And how did you and Daddy become my parents?"

"Well . . ."—I scanned the archives of my memory for advice I've read by and for adoptees on how best to proceed—"you were a surprise to Michele. Before she even knew she was pregnant, you were being born."

"Uh huh," Reed said, encouraging me. He'd heard his story before.

"She was going to college and wasn't really prepared to take care of *any* baby right then. She had to scramble to figure out how to do that—take care of a baby while finishing up school. She tried really hard, and she loved you very much, but she just couldn't figure out how to be a mom right then."

"Did you know her before that?" my son asked.

"No. We met her after she went to the same agency we did and picked us to be your forever parents."

"When did you meet her?"

"The first time we met it was just Michele and Daddy and me at the agency. It was a time for her to check us out. It was a big decision for her, and she took it very seriously. *Who* could she entrust her beloved son to? The agency called us later that evening to say that Michele had decided on us and that we could come back the next day to meet our son. And bring him home."

I paused to read his body, still nestled against mine. I knew that he was present with me, with the story.

"The next day we drove back to the agency, but this time Grandma and Grandpa and Tessa were also invited. It was the first time we saw you, and, boy, were we happy! You were so adorable and loveable. Michele brought her three best friends. We all met in a conference room for an entrustment ceremony."

"What's that?"

"That's where Michele entrusted you into our care."

"Tell me about that."

"Well . . ." I knew that this coming part was likely to hurt. I breathed and became conscious of my breath. "Michele was holding you. The lady running the meeting said a prayer for Michele and a prayer for AJ (who wasn't able to be there). There was a prayer for Daddy and me and, of course, a prayer for the baby—you—who joined everyone in the room together."

"Then what?"

I breathed again. "Then Michele placed you in my arms."

My son then let out one whimper. His small body sobbed one time. I held him more tightly (but not too tight) and stroked his shoulder, arm, side, leg. "I know, baby." I breathed deeply, willing him to, as well.

I abided with him for a moment, simply giving him the space to feel what he was feeling. Then his sister Tessa entered the room and asked what we were talking about and would I tell her about her story, too?

The next day Reed and I ran some errands. I aimed to get back into the emotional space we'd been in the night before.

"So, remember last night? We were talking about the moment when you became our son. You seemed sad. Do you want to talk about that?"

"I dunno. It's just that I was sad for Michele. No one wants to give away their baby."

"That's so right. It was very hard for Michele to do that. But what about you? What do you suppose that moment felt like for you?"

Now, some would be content to leave this stone unturned, thinking that not everything has to be dealt with. But my view is that what lies dormant affects us unconsciously and what is brought to the surface can be felt, examined, and released. My hope is that if my son can become aware of his emotions and motivations at age eight then maybe they won't get buried over the decades and erupt for him massively later in life. I want to give my children a head start on living mindfully, consciously.

My lofty goals don't mean, however, that Reed was ready to feel the emotions from the moment when he was placed in my arms by the woman who was his first mom.

"I think I had a poopy diaper and I wanted it changed," he laughed a jittery laugh, not quite ready to Go There.

"You're silly," I said and laughed with him, giving him space and not filling the silence that followed.

Soon he continued, "I probably wanted milk. I had gotten milk from my mom, and now I wanted milk from my new mom." We both sat with that. A few blocks passed in silence.

"You know," I resumed, "that moment when I became your mom was such a strange time. Everyone in the room was feeling something very intensely. For Michele, it was one of the saddest and hardest days of her life. For Daddy and Tessa and me, it was one of the happiest. Isn't that strange?"

"Yeah. I'm sad for Michele. No one wants to give away their baby." He repeated this, trying on his first mom's feelings.

"That's so very true. Especially a baby as wonderful as you, Reed."

"Mom, do her children ever ask about me?" Reed has a younger half-brother and half-sister who had visited the summer before.

"I would imagine they ask about you, or they will when they are old enough to understand."

"But what if they don't know about me? What if she doesn't tell them?"

"I'm sure she's not hiding you. After all, they've been to our house once and hopefully they'll come again. I think she's very proud of the young man you're becoming. She keeps up with you on my Facebook page, you know."

"Mom. Would you adopt another baby?"

"We don't have plans to do that. Is that something you'd like?"

"Yeah," he said, thinking. "I want to know what it felt like for Tessa when I joined the family.

I suspect this is also because he has missed out on the big-brother experience with Michele's two parented children and AJ's new baby daughter.

"I'm not sure that's likely to happen. You'll get to be the big cousin to Aunt Tami's baby when she's born."

"*Not* cousin. I want to be the big brother to a baby."

"I'm sorry, Reed."

We had arrived at our destination.

Later that night I pulled down a small item from the very top of Reed's bookshelf. It was a brilliant little present to me, to us, from the me of 2003.

Right before I had headed to the entrustment ceremony to meet and bring home our son, I had the flash of insight to bring a blank spiral journal I'd had lying around. I asked Michele after the ceremony to write a page to Reed, to tell her what was in her heart for him that day, what her hopes were for him.

I, too, put my thoughts down in that notebook frequently in those early days, and I recruited Roger, my parents, and everyone who attended Reed's first several birthday parties to write him words of love. We ended up with a couple dozen pages of people just loving on Reed over the years, until about 2006, when we moved and the book got put away.

At bedtime, Reed was able to read the time-capsule message from his birth mom. He slept with that notebook that night.

So what can be gleaned from these conversations with my son?

1. *Know what it was and what it wasn't.* The questions Reed asked and the things he said in his wondering about Michele didn't hurt me at all (other than the fact that he was hurting). Why? *Because none of it was about me.* This knowing is what enables me to be fully present for my children during such times. This point is key for adoptive parents to get, deep down in our bones. This was about my son and his innermost feelings. He will have them whether or not I am comfortable with him having them. The

question is, can he trust me enough to express his innermost feelings with me?

2. *Become impervious.* Allow, encourage, enable your kids to feel their feelings about their birth families, and do it imperviously, as you do when discussing other hurts they might have that also have nothing to do with you: a broken toy, being spurned by a friend, not making the team. The feelings about birth parents are likely more intense, but they are no more about you than these other scenarios are. The questions and wondering about the birth family are not about you and therefore take away nothing from you. Take yourself out of the equation and it becomes so much simpler.

3. *The myth of strength.* I am not any stronger than any other parents. It's just that I get, deep in my bones, #1 above.

4. *Don't dread having these conversations with your child . . .* because, well, see #1. Why not decide to enjoy rather than endure these moments of adoptive parenting? Opening your heart sets you up for true intimacy much better than will gritting your teeth.

5. *Don't dread your child having these feelings, either.* If your child doesn't encounter these emotions, great. If he does, however, why psych yourself out ahead of time? Besides, why would you want to deprive your child of all the soul deepening and self-knowledge that comes from having feelings, which we label as "good" or "bad" but can simply be guideposts for how to live? Do not be afraid of your child feeling his feelings; fear only his *not* feeling his feelings or getting stuck in them. Help your child keep the emotions in motion. It's the repression and stagnancy that cause problems.

6. *Get to know.* How did I figure out #1? By listening to adult adoptees. If you seek out blogs or books by adult adoptees, don't internalize everything you read, but do be on the lookout for gems that will help you understand what may one day be felt by your child, as well as the underlying reasons.

7. *Don't underestimate the strength of your child.* A wise man (alright, my husband, a K–12 educator) tells me that a child will rise or fall to the level of expectation you set. Notice the strength of my son in these two conversations. He has all that within him. I just held the expectation that he would tap it. If your child's story has some difficult components to it, then when you do talk about the hard stuff, envelop him in love and be open to deep wisdom. Also, see the strength and resilience of your child. He needs to see you reflect back to him those traits he already has.

It is my belief that most anyone strong enough to survive infertility and the adoption process and to undertake parenting is able to rise to adoptive-parenting moments like these. You may be surprised at what capabilities lie within you.

DIY

This has been a do-it-yourself chapter, with insight and possible solutions to common hitches that have ready answers. Sometimes, though, we are faced with bigger jobs that need a professional with more tools on the tool belt. Should you find yourself in a relationship problem that you can't seem to work through, or if your child begins to have difficulties that you aren't able to resolve by tuning in and giving space, it may be best to seek professional care. Information on finding an adoption-competent therapist can be found in the appendix.

LOOKING FORWARD TO LOOK BACKWARD

When planning a trip to a destination you won't reach for a decade or two, it's helpful to keep your eyes on the prize, what you want the results of your efforts to look like. The letter you wrote to your future adult child in the last chapter? Let it guide you through rough parenting moments, like a beacon in a storm.

8

OPENNESS IN FOSTER, INTERNATIONAL, AND DONOR SITUATIONS

For all the reasons that openness can facilitate integration between a child's biology and her biography in matched newborn adoptions, openness can likewise help children parented though foster adoption, international adoption, and donor situations do the same. When contact is available and prudent, openness can mean actual contact. When contact is either not possible or not wise, openness may mean simply a way of talking about and working though adoption issues together with your child.

FOSTER ADOPTION AND OPENNESS

Dealing with parents who voluntarily place a child is one thing. Dealing with parents who lose their parental rights is another. One difference is choice—some birth parents in the foster system may feel as if they had no choice in the relinquishment and may have a different grieving path than do placing parents in a domestic infant adoption. Another difference is the age of the child, which may range from newborn to teenager, as well as the contact and experiences that the child has had with her biological family. A third difference is the uncertainty. Reunification between a biological parent and child is highly sought whenever possible, which can leave foster parents in limbo longer than in domestic infant-adoption situations.

Despite these differences, many core issues remain the same. Mary Memmott, who blogs at *Adoption and Foster Care: My Personal Experiences*, shares her initial thoughts about fostering and openness:

> Next to the pain of reunifications, interacting with the parents of children who have come into foster care was probably the next biggest concern my husband and I had when we were first considering fostering. Much of our concern had to deal with safety and privacy issues—because the thought of interacting with people who have criminal histories or ties to drugs and gangs isn't something we exactly want to welcome into our family and personal life. Neither was the thought of working with people who abuse or neglect their children. Needless to say, when comparisons and judgments arise—because they inevitably will—it's far too easy (either consciously or unconsciously) to develop a sense of superiority between myself as a foster parent and the bio parents of the foster children in my care. After all, I bake *cookies* in my kitchen—not meth. I'm not one of *those* parents.[1]

Mary goes on to reflect on the human tendency to judge and feel superior:

> It can be far too easy for others (myself included) to judge birth parents of foster children and have an attitude of smugness or to lean much more toward justice than mercy when considering their situation. After all, they're adults and should be held accountable for having their kids taken away in the first place, right? But two things I've learned as I've gotten to know my foster children's parents are:
>
> 1. People generally do the best they know how. If someone has grown up with violence in the home, or if their parents abused and neglected them as a child, it can be extremely difficult to break that cycle, *or* they may not realistically know any different way of parenting because they haven't had the opportunity to see another kind of modeling.
> 2. Even the most upstanding citizen or model parent can drastically change if they become enslaved by addiction.[2]

Mary reveals how she moved from judgment to compassion and was able to put each of her foster children at the center of her decision making, regarding openness. She says that "a huge part of learning to accept and even show respect toward others (especially when you don't agree with them or have a hard time understanding them) is to put yourself in their shoes and try to see things from their perspective. . . . When birthparents and foster parents can put differences aside and work together out of a shared concern for a child, then everyone benefits—not just the caregivers, but caseworkers and, most importantly, the child."[3]

Melissa, an adoptive mom in Colorado, finalized her foster adoption of two children after fostering five others who were eventually reunified with their biological families. She talks about balancing safety and connection:

> From the beginning of my foster-to-adopt journey, I have tried to focus on compassion toward the biological families involved. Throughout our training, emphasis was placed on the importance of keeping positive connections intact (if and when possible), and I wholeheartedly agree. Of course, my concern above all else is for the safety and well-being of my children. Every case is different, and there is no one way of doing it.
>
> The siblings I had the honor of adopting have few bio family members I consider safe and healthy. I'm neither being selfish nor controlling, as I discussed my opinions with social workers and others close to the case and they agreed. There are several bio family members who are a safety threat to us. As a mother, I will have none of it. Some are incarcerated for now, and, trust me, I do keep close tabs.
>
> My children have an older half-sibling who was adopted by paternal grandparents, and these three are the only ones we have maintained a healthy relationship with. They are removed from the core drama, and I have faith they will keep our information confidential. Keeping contact is worth the effort, because the children have always had a close bond with their older brother. My children adore him, and vice versa. Although when the children are together some old wounds are opened, the healing eventually comes. At least we can walk through it together, and that, to me, is what family is all about.[4]

Rachel Hoyt, MSW, has worked in a foster-and-adoption program in Illinois since 2002. She shares some of her observations about the children in foster-adoption cases:

If open adoptions are about the children, why does it matter what issues their birth parents have? Does the fact that their mother has a substance-abuse issue mean that a child won't want to know them? Does the fact that their father is in jail negate a child's need to understand why they aren't being raised by them?

Children who were adopted from foster care deserve to maintain connections with their biological families. Many of these children lived with their biological parents for some time and already have attachments, however disrupted, to these parents. Even if they do not, they are no different than a child whose parent made a thought-out plan to place them for adoption. They will need the same answers and have the same desire to know their birth families.[5]

In the 2009 film *The Blind Side*, we see the pull that the mother has on Michael Oher, despite her addiction issues. Michael is known by caseworkers as a "runner" who eventually leaves each of his foster homes to return to the projects and check on his mother. Sandra Bullock's character, Leigh Anne Tuohy, understands Michael's deep-seated love and need for his mother and never makes his longing about herself. She adds herself into his life without having the need to subtract Michael's mother; she honors their bond and, rather than castigate the woman, treats her with compassion.

Rachel wonders what effects a foster parent's negative judgment about and rejection of biological parents can have on a child:

What does this teach children? That you reject people who make poor choices? That family is family only if you never have problems? How can we ask these children to trust us to love them when they make bad decisions? What if they grow up and struggle with mental health issues, substance abuse, or the like?

I have known many, many biological parents who will never be able to parent their children. They abuse drugs, they manipulate, they spend half their time in jail, they sell their bodies for basic needs, they lie, they steal, they make promises they can't keep. They are still human. They are humans who have been really, terribly hurt. But they are still parents, parents who have feelings about their children. They still deserve to know that their kids are okay.

But, more importantly, their children deserve it too. They deserve to know their parents wanted them, even if they fought in ways that were manipulative and unproductive. They deserve to know their parents are okay, even if that just means they are still alive and have enough to eat. They deserve to know that their parents do think about them and want contact with them, that they weren't thrown away and forgotten.

They deserve to know that family is family . . . no matter what.[6]

I asked Rachel how she counsels her foster-family clients around safety issues.

First, I ask the parents to take a good look at what safety means to them. Often they'll generalize and say that if a biological parent is a drug addict or has been in jail or is mentally ill then that person is obviously not safe—duh. But when I press to find out what their fears are, they have less to do with what the bio parent might *do* and more to do with what the bio parent *is*. Often we discover that the bio parent is quite capable of being clean or of staying on the appropriate medications for a meeting, of holding it together during the time she or he is with the child.

Unpredictability is something different. Bio parents are known to cancel meetings at the last minute or, worse yet, not show up, perhaps because they knew they couldn't hold it together. Unpredictability can be really hard on a family—both the foster parents and the child. But unpredictability isn't the same as unsafeness. I simply want my clients to label accurately what their concerns are and make decisions about openness accordingly.[7]

Knowing that contact isn't always possible in foster-adoption cases I asked Rachel what parents can do to create an open atmosphere sans contact. She believes that through openness, even a child who has experienced trauma can experience wholeness.

It is important that adoptive parents maintain a "spirit of openness"—bringing up the biological family and allowing the child space to talk about the good and bad of living with them (and not living with them). Too often such parents are scared of bringing up the child's past, because there can be abuse or neglect that the child can remember. But if a child is allowed the space to think and talk about those memories, she will often come up with positive things that happened with her first family, too. Helping a child to come to terms with the good *and* bad things that happened is key to supporting her in gaining understanding and acceptance about why she is not with her biological family. It also helps her to understand the big picture about the issues their biological parents struggle with and will hopefully allow her to separate her parents' issues from her own self-worth.

It's imperative that adoptive parents work through their own anger and frustration with the biological parents' actions and issues, because they will need to help their child understand them one day. A child who was born to parents with substance-abuse issues will need to understand the hold that drugs and alcohol can take on a person so that they do not believe "If I were better/smarter/better behaved" their parents would have been strong enough to give up their addictions. A child who was born to parents with mental illness needs to understand that just like a person cannot will away cancer, their parents could not will away their mental-health problems. It is also important to remember that some of these issues have genetic predispositions, which the adopted child should know about so that she can make choices about how to lead her life (being more diligent about drinking or experimenting with drugs, being more aware of their mental health and seeking support early if symptoms arise, etc.).

Adoptive parents should offer space for the child to talk about the pain and trauma caused by living with their biological families (or sometimes with previous foster families). But it is also important that they be allowed to talk about the positives, even if those positives are a bit exaggerated by time or fantasy. Having a realistic yet compassionate attitude about the child's biological family maintains the "spirit of openness" even if actual contact is not possible.[8]

Rachel says that the tenets of openness in adoption are slowly seeping into the world of foster adoption: moving from an either/or model to an and/both model, the way it was depicted in *The Blind Side*; normalizing biological relationships as much as possible, including extended family members; talking openly and honestly and age-appropriately to your child about his story. In the coming years, Rachel predicts, we'll see caseworkers better trained to counsel their clients how to parent with more openness.

INTERNATIONAL ADOPTION AND OPENNESS

International adoptions were once thought of as the most closed of the closed adoptions. After all, sheer distance, not to mention difficulties in finding and connecting with birth family members, made contact a long shot in most cases. Many also face a language barrier. But the Internet as a connecting tool and evolving views on openness are prompting more and more adoptees and their families to seek more contact than was once possible.

Kate Kaufman Burns, MSW, LCSW, and executive director of the Adoption Resources and Counseling Center in Clifton Park, New York, speaks about the gift of openness in international adoptions:

> Just as in domestic adoptions, many believe that the gift of any degree of openness is three-fold: it helps to minimize a child's loss of relationships, it helps maintain and celebrate a child's connections with all the important people in his or her life, and it allows children to resolve losses with truth, rather than with fantasy. And some truths are painful, some relationships are difficult, some details will forever be a mystery. Yet when it is safe to create connections for your child, openness in any adoption, however limited, can be a great gift. Regardless of the role of openness in adoption, the goal of adoptive parents continues to be to love their children unconditionally through all that is known and unknown.[9]

On the early end of the journey toward openness is Jennifer, who in 2010 adopted Ariana as an infant from Colombia in 2010.

> Openness in international adoption means, to us, raising our daughter with a keen awareness of who she is and where she came from. It means educating her brothers about their sister's cultural background. It means telling our children about Colombia and hopefully taking them to visit. It means preserving everything we have and know about Ariana's birth mother. It means teaching Ariana who this important woman is and how hard it was for her to give her up and how much she desired a better life for her daughter. It means answering any and all questions Ariana is sure to have very openly and honestly. It means supporting Ariana if she wants to know more than

the information we received. It also means being there for our daughter if she wants to find her birth mother and using all of our resources to help her. It means raising her to understand that even though we brought her up, her birth mother is part of our family because Ariana is.

To be closed about our adoption would be to ignore the incredible sacrifice that Ariana's mother made.[10]

Nancy also adopted an infant from Colombia—her son, Diego, who is now an adult in his mid-twenties.

Diego was a little boy who was always very curious about adoption, about Colombia, and about his birth mother. I remember when he was six or seven, sitting in the back seat of the car, sucking his thumb and telling me he had two mothers; he stuck up two fingers while still sucking his thumb. I nodded, and he went on to say it wasn't like Cinderella with a mean stepmother, and it was clear he was talking about me and his birth mother. Whenever he said something like that, I always accepted it as the truth because it was the truth. He may not have known his birth mother, but she was real in his heart.

When Diego began seventh grade, he had the opportunity to choose a language. He chose French. It was at a time in his life when he was sensitive about anything that made him different, and the boy who always was interested in anything Latino suddenly was not at a point where he wanted to address that part of himself. I wasn't a very pushy mother, but I told him he had to learn Spanish. I remember telling him if he ever found his birth mother I wanted to be sure he could talk to her. He switched to Spanish and looked for every opportunity to improve his Spanish skills. By the end of high school he was fluent in Spanish, which made a huge difference when he found his birth mother. He often tells me that he knows many adoptees who found their birth parents and he has had the most satisfying experience of any he has heard. He has a friend who found her birth mother right before she died, others found someone it was harder to connect with.

Diego was lucky. He and I went together to meet his birth mother and her two daughters and her brother. She had never told anyone about Diego, but it was clear she always thought about him and she was grief stricken every October [around Diego's birthday], which her daughters never understood. When he found her, it was as if some weight was lifted from her shoulders. He has been back to

Colombia a few times since that first visit and each time has more opportunity to develop a fuller relationship. He Skypes with them regularly. He now has met his birth father, his paternal grandparents, and a paternal uncle who lives in Florida with whom he is very close and who he visits every year or two.

After Diego first met his birth mother, he said that all the things about himself which seemed so random suddenly made sense. I know that finding his birth family has made him more comfortable with himself and more comfortable with his parents. We are lucky that he shared this journey with us right from the beginning, which helped us feel closer to him.[11]

Judy Miller adopted her daughters from China and her son from Guatemala. Birth-family contact has not been possible for any of her children, but Judy reveals how she provides openness nevertheless.

Openness in international adoption means that I own my parenting role and all of the responsibility it encompasses. Openness means confronting any fears—about the known and unknown facts about my children's histories—and how they (and all of us) might be affected by those facts. Openness begs that I grow to become a fully capable, communicative, empathetic, and supportive parent in order to best help my children navigate their journeys. Openness requires that I fully embrace faith and parenting with grace. Openness means that I be child-centered while still attending to my spouse's and my needs, as individuals and as a couple, understanding that parenting adopted children often requires much more of us. As a result our kids feel comfortable talking about their feelings; they feel validated, supported, safe, and appreciated.[12]

Motivation to bring about openness can come from the pull of the child as well as compassion for the first parents. Jessica O'Dwyer, author of *Mamalita: An Adoption Memoir*, explains her journey toward openness in adoption.

My two children were born in Guatemala—Olivia in 2002 and Mateo in 2004. The more I became my children's mother, the more I thought about their other, first, mothers. Wouldn't those unknown women wonder about the babies they gave birth to? Wouldn't they want to know that those babies were alive and healthy, cared for and loved?

During our kids' adoption process, the United States required a DNA match between birth mother and child, a cheek swab of tissue to prove a genetic link. When I received the DNA test results for Olivia, the file included two photos of our daughter sitting on her birth mother's lap. Seeing them together, the way they looked so much alike—the narrow shape of their faces, their intensely black hair, their dark brown skin—and the way neither one of them looked anything like me . . . that experience shook me to the core.

For my children, too, a connection to their birth mothers felt vital. Indeed, what are the big questions we all grapple with? *Who am I? Where do I come from?* Internationally adopted kids ask those questions, and instead of answers they find only mystery. To help fill in those blanks, we hired professional searchers in Guatemala to look for our children's birth mothers. I tell about this quest in *Mamalita*.

Yes, struggles remain—questions about why they were relinquished while other children were not, painful feelings of loss and abandonment, sadness about their families' situations. Nevertheless, establishing and maintaining contact with [the birth families], and going to Guatemala to visit and see and touch one another in person, has been overwhelmingly positive for my children. I describe it as a circle being closed.

Other adoptive parents ask me, *Don't you feel threatened? Don't you feel your kids will love you less?* The exact opposite is true. Knowing my children's birth mothers has extended our family, enlarged it. We have more people to love.[13]

Lisa Schuman, LCSW, is a psychotherapist in New York City who specializes in adoption and infertility. She has witnessed many families' attempts to practice openness in both foster and international adoptions and has this to say:

Any type of openness can continue to foster good feelings, a continual understanding of their child, information the child may need, and opportunities to see good things in the birth parent that can, when appropriate, be communicated to the child and help the child to feel whole and good, in every inch of themselves. And although the child's primary influence is the parent(s), the birth parents are still part of him. Regardless whether that part is small or large, it exists, and any good experiences parents can convey will also ultimately help reinforce to the child that those aspects of himself are good as well.[14]

That's a worthwhile goal for any parent to have.

DONOR EGGS, SPERM, EMBRYOS, AND OPENNESS

People take the donor gamete/embryo path for various reasons—single parenthood, same-sex couplehood, the wish for a couple to contribute half the DNA when possible, and the desire to experience pregnancy, to name a few. The commonality with adoption remains the same. The resulting child will have a biological connection to a parent who is not raising her. More and more, openness with gamete and embryo donors is not only possible but desirable.

Kami has two daughters via donor eggs. Openness can be tough, she says, but she does it anyway:

> I talk openly about the donor conception to others with my children around, and I also talk directly to them about it. I have found it is much harder than I expected. I sometimes don't like to think about them not being my genetic children. But more than that, how to explain to a four year old what conception is, never mind donor conception?
>
> Knowing that four years is that magic time when they need to already know so they don't remember getting told, I once tried to explain donor conception to my older daughter by comparing their coming-into-being to that of their cousins. To my ears, it sounded like I was saying, "You aren't like 'normal' people." I don't think it made any sense to them at all. Since then, I have backed off and am hoping that more casual, everyday stuff that can come up will be sufficient. We talk about babies growing in mommies, we talk about Baby Sister being in the freezer before she grew in my uterus. And sometimes we talk about that "special lady" named Belinda who helped us out. We now see her about once a year.[15]

Kami admits that she still struggles with remnant grief from her infertility struggle but that she strives to keep her issues *her* issues and not her daughters'.

> Sometimes I wish they were our mutually genetic children. I envy people who had fertility issues but then were able to have their mutually genetic children. It seems then the past could be complete-

ly forgotten. Perhaps if we decided to keep the donor conception a secret we could have forgotten the past too. I could completely bury the sting I feel sometimes when I think about another person contributing to my daughters' genetic makeup and having such a tremendous impact [on] who they are. But to do that would not be honest—to myself or to them. Even though it wasn't my first choice, and even though it still hurts sometimes, these issues pale compared to the joy [our children] bring us and the love we have for them.[16]

Kami follows the No Big Deal approach, hoping that by normalizing the details of conception and by having casual contact with their biological mother, her girls will feel as if coming into the world via donor eggs is not odd.

I hope one day my girls will be glad they have access to their genetic contributor. I hope they will think their special conception is no big deal. I hope they will know how much I love them just the way they are.

We are still early in our journey, and don't know how I am doing. Right now I am just feeling my way along and am currently happy with the go-with-the-flow approach. Bottom line, it is better to let them grow up with the knowledge, however clumsily delivered, than to put them in a situation where they have to redefine themselves upon learning at a later date.[17]

Mothers aren't the only ones who must come to terms with having no genetic connection to a child. Eric Schwartzman discovered shortly before his wedding that he suffered from male-factor infertility. Eric now manages a Yahoo! group for donor-insemination dads and shares his story of parenting a son and a daughter, thanks to one sperm donor.

Openness means that my children can always know from where they started, even if they may not have every fact about their donor. It means there are no secrets between me and them as to why we used donor conception to bring them into the world. I have read about and met too many young people who, while they love their parents (bio and nonbio), they still feel betrayed by a process that they believe robbed them of the truth of who they are. Openness means my kids will have a shot at not feeling different from other kids or that their story is anything to be ashamed of or kept locked up. It is part of who they are, but how they build upon that is up to them.

We promote openness by acknowledging the donor and the role he played. My kids know their story. They don't go telling everyone, as it is a personal one, but they know any questions they have they can always ask. We have found or been contacted by the only two half-siblings we know about and who found us via the Donor Sibling Registry. We have met both kids and spent parts of various vacations visiting with each so the kids know there are others like them, related to them, that they can turn to and just have fun with. How they develop these relationships as they grow up is up to them. My son knows he has two classmates just like him. Do these kids talk about this stuff? I don't know, but knowing they are not alone is something they can use when they want to.

The benefit to openness is that there are no secrets hiding in plain sight, no worries about what they may learn and could resent being withheld from them. The difficulties are the worries about what unknown medical conditions may exist in the donor's background that were not reported in his bio or not screened for by the clinic. These were risks we accepted when we chose this path. And it is the not knowing that makes me wonder with possible guilt about what may be lurking in their genes. But you end up trusting that the right decision was made and go with faith, as otherwise the not knowing could drive you nuts.

I hope my kids will understand that the decision to use donor conception was a choice not to side step the pain of infertility and to push off questions and pain onto them, but that two parents made a decision and they tried to be honest and be there for two children they loved. I hope they will say even though I was not biologically their father that I was the best dad I could be to them and that they always knew how much I loved them.[18]

I asked Eric if he had any advice for parents via donor sperm, egg, or embryo who sought openness. "Get involved," he said. "Ask questions. Read both [the procontact and anticontact] points of view, and understand that there are those who don't believe in openness. But think about it from the point of view of the kids and what you would want to know. With openness there are no secrets, and when there are no secrets every step is taken together. And respect is given by trusting each other that we are trying our best."[19]

ISSUES: WE ALL HAVE THEM

If you come to parenting via any of the methods discussed in this chapter, your child may face issues besides the usual growing-up ones. There may be past or current trauma, issues of identity formation, cultural- or ethnic-integration issues, feelings of differentness and otherness, and a need to gather together all the pieces and discover how to fit them together to make a self. The child does not need to also deal with adult issues that parents might have, which include denial of the existence of other parents, anger or competition with the other parents (the actual biological parents or the "ghost" parents, the ones imagined at times), or unresolved grief over the lack of a biological connection.

Growing up is hard under the best of circumstances, and issues abound any way you look at it. Leave your child to deal with only his and not yours.

THE TOUR IS ALMOST OVER

We've traveled almost 360 degrees around our subject, this thing we call open adoption, and viewed it from many perspectives. Coming up is a chapter devoted to birth parents and those who want to connect more closely with them.

9

ESPECIALLY FOR BIRTH PARENTS (AND THOSE WHO WANT TO CONNECT WITH THEM)

My dad taught my sisters and me that any happy relationship requires each person to give in two-thirds of the time. We mocked him at this statement—we knew the math didn't add up.

His point was that humans tend to overestimate their own contributions to harmony and underestimate everyone else's. With such subjective measures, a commitment from each party to giving in two-thirds of the time is a good way to make efforts meet. This suggestion works for siblings, for partners, and for adoptive and birth parents.

Frequently we hear from adoptive parents, "But we're doing *our* part—why doesn't someone tell the birth parents that *they* need to work at this open thing too?"

The thing is, most birth parents do. And in general, people usually do the best they can. In this chapter we'll cover some issues specific to first parents, such as their responsibilities in the relationship, the stumbling blocks they might face, and ways a birth parent can ask for more openness. We'll also address what adoptive parents wish they could tell their child's birth parent and how an adoptive parent might appeal to an absent birth parent for more contact.

CRYSTAL SAYS: What is my part in making this open adoption work?

I give Lori and Roger open and honest communication. I love them, and I always treat them with respect. I'm mindful of my own feelings so they don't jump out and surprise me, and I also try to figure out how Lori and Roger might feel in a given situation.

At the same time, we don't get into each other's heads. If I have an assumption about something, like a birthday party, I check that assumption with Lori. I respect that she's Tessa's mom. It also helps that we are on the same parenting page. I see Lori doing a wonderful job raising Tessa, providing her with lots of guidance and patience and linking behavior with consequences.

It takes two to set boundaries, but when you're focused on the same thing it's easier. *I* knew what I wanted for Tessa and *Lori and Roger* knew what they wanted for Tessa. Luckily, our desires for her overlap well.

Our open adoption is clearly working for Tessa. I would never consider dishonoring our relationship with disrespect, with holding a grudge, or with not being clear in myself and with her parents. If I did, it would negate the sacrifice I made for Tessa in placing her with them.

Like any good relationship, ours works because we all *want* it to work and are willing to *do* the work. And because Tessa is at the center of it. I'm so happy, though, that we genuinely like each other, too.

I wish I could do everything in life as gracefully as I've done this open adoption.

RESPONSIBILITIES

Not surprisingly, the responsibilities of a first parent look a lot like the responsibilities of an adoptive parent. Why? Because these are the basic ingredients required for most well-functioning relationships, adoptive or not: respect, honesty, clear communication, compassion and empathy, clarity, respect for reasonable boundaries, setting reasonable boundaries for one's self, an eyes-on-the-prize focus, and grace. Crystal encompasses these responsibilities in her reflection on the relationship between birth parents and adoptive parents.

HITCHES FOR BIRTH PARENTS

In chapter 7 we covered some of the Buts that can be experienced by adoptive parents and adopted children in an open adoption. Let's address now the hitches that can come up for birth parents.

But wouldn't it be better for my child and his new family if I just disappear and let them move on? Wouldn't that allow them to have a normal life?

Adoption is an alternative way to build a family, but it's not abnormal. Living a normal life means we live the life we have and not the life we *think* we should have. Looking at it this way, your presence in your child's life may actually be one of the more effective ways to normalize things for your child.

But I am angry! Angry at my parents, angry at my church, angry at the other birth parent, angry at the people who are parenting my child, angry at God—Just. Plain. Angry at being in this position.

Even when an expectant parent freely chooses adoption as the best of available options (and especially if he or she doesn't choose freely) there can be anger at being in the situation in the first place and at the lack of reinforcement offered by loved ones and support systems. Anger can manifest as depression and can fester if not dealt with. It's no surprise that such a huge loss could engender big emotions. Often it's wise to get professional help so that you can move through the anger and sadness to find how to function and move forward not only with your life but possibly also being part of the child's life. If you had an adoption social worker, ask for ongoing counseling or, at the least, for a list of affordable mental health resources. Alternatively, conduct an

Internet search for *affordable mental health care* with and without your zip code. This way you'll find options for both online and local support.

But it hurts too much. It's just too much for me.

Again, if you feel stuck in the tough emotions, you need to get them in motion and move through them. How? Get some counseling; search the Internet for *affordable mental health care* if you don't have other resources available to you through a school, a church, a health-care plan, or other means. Some self-help measures you can take:

- *Move.* Walk, run, hike, dance, mountain bike, swim, rock climb, do martial arts or yoga or play another sport. Movement helps reverse stagnation.
- *Create.* Write, compose, paint, draw, choreograph, mix a song, rap, blow glass, make pottery, plant and tend a garden. Unleashing your creative juices will also help emotions flow through and not get stuck.
- *Connect.* Ask local adoption professionals to direct you to support groups. Find an online support group (such as Birthmom-Buds.com) or an in-person one near you. To find both online and in-person resources, try an Internet search of *birth parent support group* with and without your zip code. If you don't find an in-person group near you, why not start one, the way some birth parents did in Ohio when they organized OhioBirthParents.org? At the beginning you may be a supportee, but after a time you may find yourself a full-fledged supporter of others in need.

But I don't know what to say or how to act around my child. I'm afraid I'll be judged.

Hopefully you'll be able to develop a relationship with your child's parents in which you can (1) talk with them about your feelings and fears and (2) be yourself around them and your child. Being with your child may be awkward at first—the beginnings of relationships often are—but once you plunge in, often your fears dissolve and things work themselves out. Just showing up over and over again will help resolve this issue. If not, there's always counseling and support (see previous sections). Crystal and I have found that the fears in our heads are almost always much worse than what actually ends up happening. We've also found that the judge we fear most often is our inner critic, not anyone outside of us.

But I don't deserve to be in my child's life. I messed everything up.

Of all the people in our lives, sometimes the hardest one to forgive and show compassion for is ourself. But it's required that you do so! Self-flagellating serves no purpose. It has no benefits, only costs. And no matter what you think you do or don't deserve, your child deserves to have the pieces of himself that come from you, the pieces that only you can provide.

But I'll have to justify the adoption to my child one day.

You likely will. But if you're having the conversation with a person that you've been in contact with for years, as he's grown to the point of asking the question you're more likely to be asked to *explain* than to justify. If he comes to you one day with questions of the hows and whys of his birth and adoption, you will be merely helping your son process his story and integrate his pieces. If he comes to you one day as a stranger or as a new acquaintance, you may lack a level of intimacy with each other that allows for easy dialogue, and your story could, then, seem more like justifying than explaining. If this is your fear, then openness will actually help prevent the problem.

But what if my child's parents close the adoption some day? It will kill me.

This is, perhaps, the number one fear expressed by birth parents, and it stems from a sense of powerlessness. Adoptive parents would do well to remember that same sense of powerlessness they may have endured in the days or weeks between the match or placement and the legal relinquishment—and respond with compassion. It's a tough space to live in, and empathy is in order.

Fortunately, much of what we fear most never comes to pass. It was once pointed out to me that worrying makes us experience our fear at least one extra time than we need to, if not more. If the Bad Thing does happen, then we experience it in reality *but we also experienced it over and over in our minds.* If the Bad Thing never happens, *we have nevertheless experienced it over and over in our minds.* If your logic tells you your child's parents likely would not close the adoption, work on breathing through your fears as they arise.

If your rational mind or intuition tells you the adoption is at risk of closure, try to look at the relationship from the viewpoint of the adoptive parents. What is working well, and what isn't? Are there any misunderstandings you need to address? What are you able to do to make this relationship work better?

It can be difficult to find the words to ease a tense situation. Some people communicate better in writing (or at least a draft), because it helps bring clarity and can be reworked and refined until the message is just right. If you are heading into a conversation, you may want to write your thoughts down first to figure out what you are really trying to say, to bring forethought to getting the words out and narrow down your core message. Then you can proceed either in writing an e-mail or a letter, making a phone call, or having a talk via Skype or in person.

Like we've said before, you do what you can, and you let go the rest—you have the courage to change what's in your power to change and the serenity to accept what is not.

As in chapter 7 for adoptive parents and to adoptees, here we have addressed hitches that have do-it-yourself solutions. If you find yourself with bigger hitches in your adoption journey, professional help may be needed (see resources).

HOW A FIRST PARENT CAN ASK FOR MORE OPENNESS

If you, a first parent, find yourself in a closed or closing adoption, here is a template for how you might ask for more openness. You may change the words to fit your specific circumstances, but this gives you a start to get across your main ideas.

Dear _____,

a. I have been feeling a little concerned lately that we are losing some of the openness in our adoption relationship. Let me tell you why this concerns me. *Or* . . .
b. I have been doing some adoption reading and would like to bring up with you the subject of more openness in our relationship. Let me tell you why this interests me and why I think it would be helpful to Ben.

People sometimes assume that an open adoption is something you do for me, the birth parent. While that *is* great for me, what I'm finding out is that open adoption is really beneficial for the child—for the son we are both connected to. Here are some of the ways that having us all in his life can help Ben:

- He will have the love of not only *you*, his everyday parents who take care of him and love him and are so important to him, but also love from *me*, the mother who nurtured him before he was born [or the father who loves him, as well].
- With all of us in his life he will have access to more of the people who make him *him*. I thought it was important for Ben to *have you* in his life, and I also think it is important to have *me* in his life. Don't you agree?
- Someday he's probably going to ask you questions about why we placed, about how we chose you to be his parents, about how we felt about him back then. Those will be tough questions for you to answer. They will be tough questions for *me* to answer, but we probably agree that I am the one who should answer them because they are about me, my recollections, my feelings. I bet you would like to be able to provide that to Ben, straight from the horse's mouth, so to speak.

- I've heard that it's tough for adopted people to not look like anyone around them. So I would like the chance to include your family in my family's lives once in awhile. This way you and Ben can hang out with my parents and siblings and get a feel for where certain traits or expressions or preferences come from. I think this will help Ben integrate all the pieces of himself.

In fact, the contact I'm suggesting isn't intended to subtract anything from you and your family. My primary goal is to add to Ben, to surround him with not only your love but also mine. I have the greatest respect for your role as his parents, and I thank you for being such a great mom and dad to him. Thank you for loving him so much that you'll give him what he needs, no matter what.

I would love to open a conversation with you about how we can both contribute what we have for Ben *to* Ben. I know you want him to experience his wholeness just as much as I do. I will call you soon to brainstorm with you what this might look like.

With respect and love,

Me

WHAT ADOPTIVE PARENTS WISH THEY COULD SAY TO THEIR CHILD'S FIRST PARENTS

There is, perhaps, an assumption that adoptive parents just wish that the birth parents would go away, that they could all move on as if the adoption happened once way back then now it's over and done. That may have been the model for adoptions in the closed era, but now that we have reemerged into the era of openness, birth parents are sometimes surprised by the welcome and connection extended to them by their child's adoptive parents. We asked adoptive parents via social media what they wish they could say to the first parents of their children, and here are several responses:

- I'm so grateful for the contact and the visits we have; I hope the connection stays strong for all involved. I was actually scared of this contact before we adopted, but now I see how it benefits us all. I am so glad I made the leap of faith, and I'm grateful our daughter's birth parents trusted us with so much as well.

- I love you. (I have never said that I love them and feel it would be very awkward for me to say it. But I'm not sure they realize how amazing I think they are.)

- There's not much that goes unsaid between us and our children's birth moms. We are so lucky to have been picked by two amazing women and talk about them every day with "our" kids. I wish that were the case with their birth dads as well, but we don't have contact yet (per their request). So I would love to tell them that we're here and waiting with open arms (patiently for now but soon to be impatiently) and they (and their parents/family) are missing out on some pretty amazing children.

- To our daughter's (so-far) absent birth father: It makes me so sad sometimes to think that she will probably grow up with almost no information about you, and I hope it doesn't cause her too much pain. We respect you, even if some of the other people around you don't treat you with much respect. We wish you'd give us a chance, for her sake.

- Please be patient with us. We're still new and learning, and this is one of the hardest relationships we have ever had to form. We're doing the best we can for her and for all of us. Please forgive us if we ever hurt you; if we did, it was unintentional. I wish you could know how deeply my heart feels the pain your decision must have caused you and that we stand in awe of your self-control and selflessness. Nothing could describe it or adequately express our gratitude.

- Your son is happy and healthy and loved beyond measure. I love being his mother more than anything else in life. I very much wish for him that you will want to connect with him at some point. You are his mother, you are where he came from, and you are part of him. He wants to know what you look like, if he looks like you, and why you are not raising him. This does not mean you made the wrong decision or that he is not a happy child. I think it means a piece of him is missing, and I cannot give him that piece. He wants to know who you are, because he wants to know who he is, all of it.

- Where did you go? Come back. Miss you.

THE RELUCTANT BIRTH PARENT

The stereotype is that it's the adoptive parents who close an adoption. But it takes two to tango, and sometimes the lukewarm—or even chilly—party in an open-adoption relationship is the first parent. Why might this happen? We've mentioned here some of the most prevalent reasons. As we've just seen in the Hitches section, there may be fear involved in contact—fear of not doing or saying the right things, fear of getting too close and feeling pain, fear of hearing the child call another woman *Mama* or another man *Daddy*. Another phenomenon we've observed is the "moving on" frame of mind, in which the first mom or dad has a template in mind for healing that means closing the door behind them in order to keep moving forward with their lives.

Adoptive parents in a formerly open adoption may never know the whys of its closing. They can, however, continue to have an open-door adoption, one in which they keep the porch light on for the time when a birth parent may want to come back. Callie explains how her open-door adoption came about:

> While we are officially in an open adoption in that we have met and know how to contact one another and we send photos, Kia did not want contact after placement. We had to respect her wishes. It's not like we have a choice—we can't *make* her be a part of our lives. We worked really hard to make a connection with her before Scott was born and while we were with her after his birth. She remained steadfast in her position, though, and we have only heard from her once since we parted ways, and that one interaction was not a comfortable

circumstance (despite it being really great before and during the adoption process).

I spent a year intensely hoping for her to call us and want to know how Scott was doing. When she did call, we saw a side of her we had not seen in our time with her before Scott was born, and while it was a very difficult time it was also liberating. I had been selfish, on Scott's behalf and on mine. I really wanted to have this terrific open adoption I had always envisioned.

But I finally realized that Kia was barely able to keep her own life together and that she had absolutely no capacity to worry about the child she gave birth to. She had already done all the worrying about him that she could in making the decision she made. So I shifted my energy to *gratitude*, a sensation for which there are no words, and for Kia to have what she needs in life to be all right. I love that woman. I cannot sufficiently express my feelings for her, and so I send her my deepest love and desire for her greatest good. And I would still welcome her if she were to feel differently in the years to come. You certainly hear about that happening.[1]

A LETTER TO GIVE TO AN ABSENT BIRTH PARENT

Earlier I provided a template for a letter that a birth parent might use to broach the subject of openness with an adoptive parent. Following is that letter's counterpart, a template for a letter to invite a first parent into the relationship. Of course, you will change it to make it your own and put it in your voice, but the main points can be delivered in this manner.

Dear _____,

I can tell you are really something special because _____ sure is. I can only imagine how difficult the thought of seeing him is for you, and I wonder if you have some fears about that. Fear that it will hurt too much to hear him call another woman *Mommy*. Fear that he will one day be mad at you. Fear that you're not deserving of seeing him. Fear that seeing you might mess him up in some way. Fear that it would hurt and never stop hurting.

But we want to ask you to consider facing these fears. We feel as if having you in _____'s life in some measure will be hugely beneficial to him. He may see his own face in your face (we hear from adult adoptees that this is a priceless gift). He will be filled with your love and care. He will have a connection with your other children, his siblings. He will eventually be able to ask questions that only you can answer. His sense of identity will be firmed up by knowing you and knowing that you love him, and that will make his teenage years a little bit easier. You may think that waiting is better for some reason, but we believe that the earlier you have a presence in his life the better off he will be. Adoption reunions between adults can be difficult, and we'd like to structure it so that there's no reunion at all, just a knowing each other from an early age.

If you would like support or counseling around coming into our lives, we will arrange for you to get that. Would you please consider opening up this adoption, for the sake of the son we both love dearly? We promise to do our best to make this not scary for you.

With respect and love,

Me

And with this, your door is open, your porch light is on, your hospitality is extended and ready to be put into service for your counterparts on this journey.

10

FARE WELL

Just like building a life has inherent risk, building an open adoption has inherent risk.[1] No one—not Oprah or Dr. Phil or Dr. Oz or *The Promise* or your counselor or your minister or your rabbi—can guarantee you that if you do what's prescribed you'll be happy. Singular human beings are infinitely complex, and relationships among these beings hold even more complexity. (See? You can go higher than infinity.) Because of so many variables and so much complexity, of course not everything will go smoothly for all people all along the way in an adoption. And, just like in life, you try to set your mesh, your screen door, so to speak, so that it lets in the good while keeping out the bad. You adjust your filter as time goes by according to events that leave an imprint on you.

What you can expect when you open your heart and mind to a reasonable relationship with your child's other parents, though, is a better chance at long-term happiness and wholeness for you and for your child. As Maya Angelou said, "I have learned that whenever I decide something with an open heart I usually make the right decision."[2]

Living in open adoption is an opportunity to move from the world of duality—either/or, black or white, good or bad, adoptive parent or birth parent, head or heart—into the realm of unity—both/and, head *and* heart. As we parents move toward this wholeness, we model for our children how to live an integrated life.

We do this for ourselves, and also for our children. They do not have to choose between their sets of parents. They have both, each with a prominent place in their lives. Biology is in the open. Biography is in the open.

And it's not a superhuman feat to open and create in such a way.

HOTEL RWANDA AND OPEN ADOPTION

A few years ago I taught world geography to middle school students. We'd done a unit on the phenomenon of genocide, and at about the same time Paul Rusesabagina came to our city for a speaking engagement. I organized a field trip, and my students and I were able to hear the first-person account of the hotel manager who'd sheltered Tutsi Rwandans during the brutal mass murders committed by their Hutu neighbors in 1994.

Truly, his story is remarkable. At risk of his safety and that of his family, Mr. Rusesabagina used his connections and wiles to save more than a thousand refugees fleeing the sectarian slaughter.

After his talk, the audience gushed praise. Each person who got up to ask a question at the end of Mr. Rusesabagina's presentation began with some version of "You are extraordinary" or "You are exceptional" or "You are amazing—I would never be able to be so brave."

With each of these proclamations, I saw Paul Rusesabagina slump a little. To each commenter he protested, "No, I'm not. My point is that I am just like you—in extraordinary times we all can be extraordinary. We *all* have it in us, and I am proof of that."

Still, the audience continued to set him apart. I left the auditorium that day feeling sad for Paul Rusesabagina, who looked a bit lonely, a bit defeated in the way his message had been received. Who, as if to make my point, titled his 2006 book *An Ordinary Man*.

But what does this have to do with open-adoption parenting?

Crystal and I have had people tell us we are "amazing" for creating the openness we have. Others who live in high-functioning open adoptions have been told they are "exceptional" or "extraordinary"—which infers that "normal" or "ordinary" people would not be able to accomplish such a feat. With such praise, you might think openness in adoption is achievable only by the godlike among us, out of the reach of mere mortals.

But, as Paul Rusesabagina said, extraordinary situations can bring out the extraordinary in all of us. Open adoption is an extraordinary situation, and it will tap into the extraordinary within you.

Don't tell me that you wouldn't run into a burning building to rescue your child. Don't tell me that you wouldn't jump in front of a bus to prevent your child from being hit. We say it all the time—this type of love transcends all. And in a moment where you're called on to do something heroic for someone you love, you would not think twice.

So why would you react any differently when it's a case of merely resolving your own fears and insecurities for the sake of your child? Over and over again, incredible, extraordinary, remarkable things are done by ordinary people.

Like you.

THE TRIP OF A LIFETIME

So there you have it, your guidebook to and through the demystified terrain of open adoption. We have covered why and how to build an open adoption. You have some ideas on what openness can look like, what is required of you, how to avoid common problems, and what to do if you come across roadblocks or sinkholes. You have begun to switch from either/or thinking to and/both thinking. You feel secure in your role in your child's life and can thus patrol your boundaries like a border collie rather than a pit bull. You realize that the clearer you can be about your fears and motivations within yourself the more adept you can be in resolving those fears with others. At the very least, you are open to being open.

Parenting itself stretches us and makes us into better people than we were before taking on such tremendous responsibility. Parenting in open adoption requires even more of us. But our children, experiencing a split at some point between their biology and their biography, need us to step up and do all we can, offer all we have, to make them whole. Once you decide to pursue wholeness for your child, you are also bringing wholeness to yourself. It may not always be easy—parenting certainly isn't, so why would parenting in adoption be any different? But one day you will look back on a very rich life in which you have lived and parented mindfully.

We wish for you peace, joy, harmony, wisdom, and wholeness as you travel the journey with your hearts open.

APPENDIX A: INSIGHT ON ADOPTION PROFILES

SEVEN TIPS TO REVIEW AND REVISE YOUR ADOPTION PROFILE[1]

What makes a profile work? I gathered anecdotal research from first parents and adoption counselors. While each first parent comes with a viewpoint as unique as a fingerprint, here are some commonalities I found in what attracts and what doesn't in a profile, distilled into seven do-it-yourself tips:

1. *Accurately represent yourselves and avoid playing to your audience.* One expectant mother might love dogs, while another might be allergic. One might want the baby to be the couple's first, while another might want ready siblings. To bring about the best match, simply be truthful about who you are and what your lives are about.

2. *Show what makes you unique.* Have a horse? Show it. Bilingual? Write a few words in another language. You want to differentiate yourselves from the others in the stack. Crystal tells me, "You proposed to Roger at a Denver Broncos game on the big scoreboard! I liked that spirit—it resonated with me."

3. *Find balance.* Describe your life as full enough that you are not dependent on a baby to make it complete yet not so full that you have no room for a child. Gwen reveals, "Both people had high-powered jobs and were involved in so many things that I just couldn't see how they'd fit in another responsibility."

4. *Inject humor.* Include an amusing anecdote or funny photo that shows that humor is one way you deal with life. "They had a picture of the whole family wearing 3-D glasses and watching fireworks," recounts first mother Kelly. "This family had a good time just being around each other."

5. *Remove all hints of desperation (by removing the desperation).* It's as much a repellent to an expectant mother as it was to a potential spouse. If you can't come by this honestly, you need more counseling before you embark on adoption. "I didn't want my baby to be the one thing that saved these people from a life of misery," explains Sarah, "so I passed on them."

6. *Be brutally honest with yourselves about your profile.* Or better yet, have a trusted friend—someone less vested in the outcome—look over your masterpiece. Ask this person to be candid about the photos, letters, and tone. Maybe you can't see that Aunt Tillie looks awful in that family photo, but you need to know. "In one picture of a family picnic, they all had red eye," explains first mother Gwen. "I know it wasn't real, but my impression was 'how demonic!'"

7. *Tinker.* Tweaking just a word or an image can dramatically change results. If you've been waiting a while, make a minor change, like the stationery or the lead photo. "If your agency is having activity but your profile isn't garnering interest, a semi-annual review with minor changes might help," suggests Karen Bettis, Adoption Counselor at Lutheran Family Services.

THE TERRIBLE TOOS: SEVEN COMMON MISTAKES IN ADOPTION PROFILES

I've reviewed dozens of adoption profiles, some in the draft stage and some that had already languished at an agency for months and months. I thought it might be helpful to reveal some of the common issues I see with ailing profiles. I call them the Terrible Toos.

1. *Too perfect.* Alan and Jackie had perfect teeth. Their parents and siblings had perfect teeth, too, *and* flawless skin. They took perfect vacations together and tended a perfectly manicured lawn. They were blessed and happy!

   Of course, they were only showing parts of themselves they deemed "acceptable." And, of course, a reader might be put off by a couple that belongs on a magazine cover. I encouraged Alan and Jackie to add dimensions to their profile by getting real and opening up about their dreams and heartaches. Three dimensions are more attractive than two. And *real* is the real draw.

2. *Too much.* This twenty-pager for Debbie and Curt went on and on. It left nothing to be revealed and came across as self-centered. Sometimes more is less, and vice versa.

3. *Too self-indulgent.* Similar to the lengthy profile is the us-us-us profile. It is a monologue rather than an invitation to a dialogue—a subtle difference.

   Sunny and Blake each wrote about themselves for several pages, not even acknowledging that there was a reader. Their narratives were not composed out of true egotism but rather just not knowing how to write about and present themselves in a conversational way.

   Once Sunny and Blake changed their approach from a book-report style to something else, their profile got noticed—and chosen.

   What was this magic style? Instead of each one telling about him- or herself (which is hard), Sunny and Blake told about each other (which is easier). Moreover, doing so invited the reader into the profile: *You should see Sunny when she's coaching soccer. The children flock to her like pigeons on breadcrumbs.* And it allowed the reader to see the couple through loving eyes.

4. *Too pretentious.* (I haven't actually seen this trait in a profile, but I bet it exists.) There's no need to show off the driving range in your back yard or your annual trips to Paris or your collection of sports cars. Such shows of wealth are not what an expectant parent finds comforting—wealth of time and love are. Plus, pretentiousness can build a barrier instead of finding common ground with your reader.

5. *Too guarded.* While there may be photos and text, the reader is left not really knowing anything about the hopeful parents.

    Gina and Ken had recently been scammed and were understandably cautious. They wanted to protect themselves from repeated heartbreak. In doing so, they built a wall to keep Bad Things out. But the funny thing about walls is that they are multipurpose. They also keep Good Things out.

    Throughout their pages it was clear that Gina and Ken didn't want to reveal too much about themselves. Reading their profile was the equivalent of trying to have a conversation with a person whose arms are tightly crossed over the chest.

    The wall was evident in the closing line of their profile: *Please contact us only if you are serious about an adoption plan.*

    Clearly, this wasn't a problem that would be solved just by wordsmithing. I counseled Gina and Ken about what a true (not-scamming) expectant parent considering adoption might be going through. We talked about the myths surrounding birth parents and what they could expect to find when working with an ethical adoption professional. A deeper understanding of their intended audience helped them to risk more revelations and invitations in their profile.

6. *Too blah.* Katie and Gil were careful not to put anything in their profile that was too anything. They were rabid Cornhusker fans but didn't want to offend anyone who might back an opposing team. They loved to ride motorcycles but didn't want to freak out

a reader who might be more cautious. They attended their church regularly but didn't want to mention it in case theirs wasn't the same faith as the readers'.

In short, Katie and Gil hid their lights under a bushel.

I interviewed them to find out what made them unique and vibrant and found the qualities mentioned above. Once they revised their profile to show themselves *out loud*, it wasn't long before their profile was chosen as the perfect match for an expectant parent.

7. *Too footloose.* Sam and Bill's profile had photos of them on a honeymoon in the Bahamas, toasting each other with umbrella drinks. There was also a photo series of them zip-lining in the cloud forest of Costa Rica and more of them scuba diving in crystal waters. To round off the seasons, they told about how they loved to ski during the weekends during the winter.

It's hard for a reader to envision Sam and Bill with a child. I asked them to tell me what their lives would look like once they had a child. With their answers, they revised their profile to reflect their future (as parents) as well as their past (as an active, spontaneous couple).

On Being Real

More than scrapbooking abilities, more than a gift with the written word, more than anything else, authenticity is the key to an adoption profile. *Show who you are.* Not who you wish you were, not who you think someone else thinks you should be, but who you are.

Imagine back when you first met your spouse. If you had misrepresented yourself just to make an initial good impression, eventually your house of cards would fall and your opportunity for love would have evaporated. It was vitally important with a partner, and it's equally important with the first parents of your future child: don't *hide* who you are but, rather, *reveal* who you are. That's how to begin an open adoption with the best chance of success and happiness.

APPENDIX B: OPENING YOUR HEART

EXERCISES TO EXPAND AND ENGAGE YOUR HEART

It's simply not possible to know all the right answers to every possible situation in an open adoption. Instead, having an open heart allows you to *find* the answers in the moment.

At the links below are exercises designed to help you open your mind and heart to your own intuitive abilities; to the wisdom of God or, the Divine; and to your child or children. These exercises, when performed routinely and mindfully, can help you connect with your inner light, to expand your heart, to realize that nothing is separate from you, to manifest peace around an issue, to become centered, to become aware of your own motivations and thoughts, to identify and release fear.

EXERCISE 1: MANIFESTING WHAT YOU WANT: CONTRACTION VERSUS EXPANSION

For explanation and an audio recording of this meditation, please visit http://lavenderluz.com/audioexercise1 or scan this code:

EXERCISE 2: PRACTICING PRESENCE

For explanation and an audio recording of this meditation, please visit http://lavenderluz.com/audioexercise2 or scan this code:

RESOURCES

BLOGS

Blogs are ever-changing. Search for *birthmother blogs, adoptee blogs, adoptive-parenting blogs, adoption blogs, open-adoption blogs*, or whatever subset of open adoption you would like to delve into. Here are some suggestions to get you started.

> *The Stirrup Queens' Adoption Room Blogroll*. www.stirrup-queens
> .com/a-whole-lot-of-blogging-brought-to-you-sorted-and-filed/
> adoption-room
> *Open Adoption Bloggers*. http://openadoptionbloggers.com/open-
> adoption-blogs/
> *LavenderLuz.com* (my blog!)

BOOKS

By or for Adoptees and Those Who Love Them

> *Becoming Patrick: A Memoir*, Patrick McMahon (2011)
> *Coming Home to Self: The Adopted Child Grows Up*, Nancy Verrier
> (2003)
> *The English American*, Alison Larkin (2009)
> *Journey of the Adopted Self: A Quest for Wholeness*, Betty Jean
> Lifton (1995)

The Mistress's Daughter, A. M. Homes (2008)

Parenting for Peace: Raising the Next Generation of Peacemakers, Marcy Axness (2012)

Pieces of Me: Who Do I Want to Be? Voices for and by Adopted Teens, ed. Bert Ballard (2009)

The Primal Wound, Nancy Verrier (1993)

Searching for Jane, Finding Myself: An Adoption Memoir, Jan Fishler (2010)

Swimming Up the Sun, Nicole J. Burton (2008)

What to Expect from Your Adopted Tween, Judy M. Miller (2011)

General Adoption

Adoption Nation: How the Adoption Revolution Is Transforming Our Families—and America, Adam Pertman (2011)

Adoption Parenting: Creating a Toolbox, Creating Connections, ed. Jean MacLeod and Sheena Macrae (2006)

The Adoptive and Foster Parent Guide: How to Heal Your Child's Trauma and Loss, Carol Lozier (2012)

Bones that Float, Kari Grady Grossman (2007)

The Family of Adoption, Joyce Maguire Pavao (1999)

Kinship by Design: A History of Adoption in the Modern United States, Ellen Herman (2008)

Mamalita, Jessica O'Dwyer (2010)

Tell Me Again about the Night I Was Born, Jamie Lee Curtis and Laura Cornell (1996)

By or for Birth Parents and Those Who Love Them

The Girls Who Went Away, Ann Fessler (2006)

The Same Smile: The Triumph of a Mother's Love after Losing Two Daughters, Susan Mello Souza (2002)

Second-Chance Mother, Denise Roessle (2011)

Waiting to Forget: A Motherhood Lost and Found, Margaret Moorman (1998)

Infertility

Inconceivable: A Medical Mistake, the Baby We Couldn't Keep, and Our Choice to Deliver the Ultimate Gift, Carolyn Savage and Sean Savage (2011)
Navigating the Land of IF: Understanding Infertility and Exploring Your Options, Melissa Ford (2009)
Sweet Grapes: How to Stop Being Infertile and Start Living Again, Jean W. Carter and Michael Carter (1998)
Waiting for Daisy, Peggy Orenstein (2007)

Open Adoption

The Best for You, Kelsey Stewart (2009)
Hospitious Adoption, Jim L. Gritter (2009)
Lifegivers: Framing the Birthparent Experience in Open Adoption, Jim L. Gritter (2000)
Making Room in Our Hearts: Keeping Family Ties through Open Adoption, Micky Duxbury (2006)
The Open Adoption Experience: A Complete Guide for Adoptive and Birth Families, Lois Ruskai Melina (1993)
Openness in Adoption: Exploring Family Connections, Harold Grotevant and Ruth G. McRoy (1998)
The Spirit of Open Adoption, Jim L. Gritter (1997)

Other Resources for Adoption Books

Creating a Family's suggested reading. www.creatingafamily.org/adoption/suggestedbooks.html
EMK Press (specializes in adoption titles). www.emkpress.com/
Insight! Open Adoption Resources and Support's suggested reading. www.openadoptioninsight.org/recommended_reading_list.htm
PACER's suggested reading. http://pacer-adoption.org/books.htm
Tapestry Books (specializes in adoption titles). www.tapestrybooks.com

CD

The 72 Varieties of Open Adoption: Which Is Yours?, Marcy Axness (1998): http://marcyaxness.com/store/#!/~/product/category= 2027251&id=13966665

COUNSELING

Child Welfare Information Gateway (part of the U.S. Department of Health and Human Services) compiled a factsheet on selecting and working with adoption therapists. www.childwelfare.gov/ pubs/f_therapist.cfm
Open Adoption Support. www.openadoptionsupport.com/ thereapist-directory.

MAGAZINES

The Adoption Magazine. www.theadoptionmagazine.com/
Adoption Mosaic. www.adoptionmosaic.org/
Adoption Today. www.adoptinfo.net/
Adoptive Families. http://adoptivefamilies.com/

ONLINE RESOURCES AND COMMUNITIES

Adoptee Rights Coalition. www.adopteerightscoalition.com/
Adoption.com. www.adoption.com/
Adoption Agency Ratings. www.adoptionagencyratings.com/
Adoption Under One Roof. http://ouradopt.com/
American Adoption Congress. www.americanadoptioncongress.org/ and www.americanadoptioncongress.org/adoption_links.php
Birth Mom Buds. http://birthmombuds.com/
The Center for Adoption Support and Education (CASE). www. adoptionsupport.org
Colorado Coalition of Adoptive Families. www.cocaf.org/
Creating a Family. www.creatingafamily.org/

Creating a Family's archive of radio shows. www.creatingafamily.
org/radioshow.html

Creating a Family's list of adoption support groups. www.
creatingafamily.org/adoption-resources/adoptionsupportgrps.
html

Donaldson Adoption Institute. www.adoptioninstitute.org/index.php

Facebook. Search for *open adoption, adoptive parents, birth mom,
adoptee, adopted,* and the like to find active groups.

*Independent Adoption Center's summary of "Research on the Im-
pact of Openness on Adoptees".* www.adoptionhelp.org/open-
adoption/research

Insight! Open Adoption Resources and Support. www.
openadoptioninsight.org/

NACAC's database of adoption support groups. www.nacac.org/
parentgroups/database.html

North American Council on Adoptable Children (NACAC). www.
nacac.org/

Ohio Birthparent Group. http://ohiobirthparents.org/

Open Adoption Support. http://openadoptionsupport.com/

Post Adoption Center for Education and Research (PACER). http://
pacer-adoption.org/

NOTES

INTRODUCTION

1. James L. Gritter, "Symposium 2011 Opening Adoption: Realities, Possibilities, and Challenges," keynote speech at Open Adoption Symposium, Richmond, Va.: Coordinators2, Inc., September 23, 2011. Elements of this chapter first appeared at *LavenderLuz.com*.

2. Cheryl Wetzstein, "Study: Families Trending toward Open Adoption," *Washington Times*, March 21, 2012, accessed March 23, 2012, www.washingtontimes.com/news/2012/mar/21/study-families-trending-toward-open-adoptions/.

3. Adam Pertman, "Study Shows Rise in 'Open' Infant Adoptions," Donaldson Adoption Institute, accessed April 8, 2012, http://adoptioninstitute.org/media/20120321_openness_release.php.

4. *Adoption triad* means the child, the birth parents, and the adoptive parents.

5. *Wikipedia*, "Open Adoption," accessed March 21, 2012, http://en.wikipedia.org/wiki/Open_adoption.

6. *Adoption constellation* is a newer term than *adoption triad* and can include extended and involved family members as well as adoption professionals who help facilitate adoptions.

7. Obviously, there may be more logistical challenges in providing openness in an international adoption, but it can be done. For a wonderfully written book about opening a Cambodian adoption, see Kari Grady Grossman's *Bones That Float* (Fort Collins, Colo.: Wild Heaven Press, 2001).

1. WHAT IS OPEN ADOPTION?

1. Portions of this chapter previously appeared in modified form at *LavenderLuz.com*.

2. Judy M. Miller, interview with Lori Holden, March 11, 2012.

3. Luna Sea, interview with Lori Holden, September 25, 2009, with passages excerpted from http://lifefromhere.wordpress.com.

4. Luna Sea, interview with Lori Holden, September 25, 2009.

5. Luna Sea, interview with Lori Holden, September 25, 2009.

6. Luna Sea, interview with Lori Holden, September 25, 2009.

7. Luna Sea, interview with Lori Holden, September 25, 2009.

8. Luna Sea, interview with Lori Holden, September 25, 2009.

9. Mac Sea, interview with Lori Holden, March 25, 2010.

2. WHAT TO CONSIDER WHEN CHOOSING AN AGENCY OR ADOPTION PROFESSIONAL

1. For information on adoption professionals relevant to your locale, check the U.S. Department of Health and Human Service's Child Welfare Information Gateway at www.childwelfare.gov/pubs/f_start.cfm#understand.

2. Adoption.com, "What Is an Adoption Agency?" www.adoptionagency. com/agencies/what-is-an-adoption-agency.html.

3. Laura Beauvais-Godwin and Raymond Godwin, *The Complete Adoption Book: Everything You Need to Know to Adopt a Child* (Cincinnati, Ohio: Adams Media, 2005), 12.

4. ChildWelfare.gov offers a comprehensive state-by-state summary of laws regarding adoption advertising and facilitation at www.childwelfare.gov/ systemwide/laws_policies/statutes/advertisingall.pdf.

5. Lori Holden, "Why I Am Pro–Open Adoption," *LavenderLuz.com*, accessed April 12, 2011, http://lavenderluz.com/2011/04/why-i-am-pro-open-adoption.

6. U.S. Department of Health and Human Services, "Regulation of Private Domestic Adoption Expenses," *Child Welfare Information Gateway*, 2010, www.childwelfare.gov/systemwide/laws_policies/statutes/expenses.pdf.

7. Stephanie Moore, interview with Lori Holden, December 20, 2011.

8. Claudia Corrigan D'Arcy, "Is Your Adoption Agency Ethical?" *Musings of the Lame: My Life as a Birthmother and What I Learned Too Late*, January 27, 2012, www.musingsofthelame.com/2012/01/is-your-adoption-agency-ethical.html.

9. Jennifer Lawlor, interview with Lori Holden, December 16, 2011.

10. Brandy Hagelstein, Domestic Adoption forums, Adoption.com, May 6, 2008, http://forums.adoption.com/domestic-adoptions/333597-adoption-application-question-regarding-birth-mother-expenses.html.

11. Ellen Roseman, interview with Lori Holden, December 16, 2011.

12. Ellen Roseman, interview with Lori Holden, December 16, 2011.

13. Robyn Chittister, interview with Lori Holden, December 20, 2011.

14. Robyn Chittister, interview with Lori Holden, December 20, 2011. For more information on state-by-state regulations about paying adoption expenses visit the Department of Health and Human Service's Child Welfare Information Gateway at www.childwelfare.gov/systemwide/laws_policies/statutes/expenses.cfm.

15. Ellen Roseman, interview with Lori Holden, December 16, 2011.

16. D'Arcy, "Is Your Adoption Agency Ethical?"

17. *Huffington Post*, "John Wyatt, Father Fights for Custody of Daughter Who Was Given Up for Adoption without Consent," October 19, 2011, www.huffingtonpost.com/2011/08/19/john-wyatt-father-fights-_n_931311.html. And find the January 19, 2011, Wyatt complaint at www.babyemmawyatt.com/wyatt.Complaint1-19-11.pdf.

3. THE PARENTS IN AN OPEN ADOPTION

1. Portions of this chapter originally appeared in altered form at *LavenderLuz.com.*

2. James L. Gritter, *LifeGivers* (Washington, D.C.: Child Welfare League of America, Inc., 2000), 152.

3. A version of this story was originally published at http://drama2bmama.blogspot.com/2009/10/adoption-school-day-2-i-am-baby.html.

4. Monika Zimmerman, interview with Lori Holden, January 4, 2012.

5. For an illuminating discussion on this topic, I urge you to listen to CreatingAFamily.com's podcast "Difficult Dialogues: The Essential Conversations That Prospective Adoptive Parents *Must* Have Before, During, and After Placement," available at http://bit.ly/M7RUuy.

6. Monika Zimmerman, interview with Lori Holden, January 4, 2012.

7. Monika Zimmerman, "A Birthmother's Perspective," *See Theo Run*, December 28, 2011, accessed January 17, 2012, http://seetheorun.com/2011/12/28/a-birthmothers-perpective/.

8. Annie, interview with Lori Holden, January 10, 2012.

9. Amy Hutton, interview with Lori Holden, February 17, 2012.

10. Annie, interview with Lori Holden, January 10, 2012.

11. That website is www.birthmombuds.com. Monika Zimmerman, interview with Lori Holden, January 4, 2012.

12. Amy Hutton, interview with Lori Holden, February 17, 2012.

13. Monika Zimmerman, interview with Lori Holden, January 4, 2012.

14. Marcy Axness, interview with Lori Holden, August 24, 2012.

15. Marcy Axness, interview with Lori Holden, August 24, 2012.

4. GUIDEPOSTS FROM FAMILIES WHO HAVE TRAVELED THE PATH

1. *Wikipedia*, "Maslow's Hierarchy of Needs," accessed February 22, 2012, http://en.wikipedia.org/wiki/Maslow%27s_hierarchy_of_needs.

2. Jim Gritter, *The Spirit of Open Adoption* (Washington, D.C.: Child Welfare League of America, Inc., 1997), 306.

3. AdoptiveFamiliesCircle.com, February 1, 2012, www. adoptivefamiliescircle.com/groups/topic/3071/.

4. Annie, interview with Lori Holden, February 21, 2012.

5. Gritter, *Spirit of Open Adoption*, 21–22.

6. Jim Gritter, *Lifegivers* (Washington, D.C.: Child Welfare League of America, Inc., 2000), 167.

7. "My Mom Tells Them How I'm Doing," February 1, 2012, www. adoptivefamiliescircle.com/blogs/post/talking-about-adoption-birth-parent-letters/.

8. "How We Got Here," *Living Through Today*, September 23, 2011, http://lisaanne119.blogspot.com/2011/09/how-we-got-here.html.

9. Meg Kenning, interview with Lori Holden, March 1, 2012.

10. See http://bit.ly/thespacebetween.

11. Meg Kenning, interview with Lori Holden, March 1, 2012.

12. Meg Kenning, interview with Lori Holden, March 10, 2012.

13. Tara, interview with Lori Holden, February 10, 2012.

14. Monika Zimmerman, interview with Lori Holden, January 4, 2012.

15. Crystal Hass, interview with Lori Holden, July 5, 2012.

16. Monika Zimmerman, interview with Lori Holden, January 4, 2012.

17. Bobbie Havens, interview with Lori Holden, February 2, 2012.

18. Bobbie Havens, interview with Lori Holden, February 2, 2012.

19. Julie Mudd, interview with Lori Holden, January 31, 2012.

20. A sample PACA can be downloaded from the Adoptive Families' website at www.adoptivefamilies.com/articles.php?aid=2035.

21. U.S. Department of Health and Human Services, "Postadoption Contact Agreements Between Birth and Adoptive Families," Child Welfare Infor-

mation Gateway, www.childwelfare.gov/systemwide/laws_policies/statutes/
cooperative.pdf.

5. OPENNESS AND THE ADOPTEE

1. Portions of this chapter originally appeared in a slightly different format at *LavenderLuz.com*.

2. Center for Adoption Support and Education, Inc., AdoptionIssues.org, accessed February 28, 2012, www.adoptionissues.org/wiseup.html.

3. Access *Adoptive Families* magazine's family-tree exercise at www.adoptivefamilies.com/school/index.php.

4. Andy Drouin, "Family Trees," *Today's the Day They Give Babies Away*, October 19, 2009, http://todaysthedaytheygivebabiesaway.blogspot.com/2009/10/family-trees.html.

5. Alicia, interview with Lori Holden, October 22, 2010.

6. Alicia, interview with Lori Holden, October 22, 2010.

7. Nancy Verrier, *Primal Wound: Understanding the Adopted Child* (Baltimore: Gateway Press, 1993), 10.

8. Maggie Macaulay, interview with Lori Holden, October 22, 2010.

9. Maggie Macaulay, interview with Lori Holden, October 22, 2010.

10. "Looking in the Mirror," *Insert Bad Movie Title Here*, February 13, 2012, http://insertbadmovietitlehere.wordpress.com/2012/02/13/looking-in-the-mirror/.

11. Torrejon, interview with Lori Holden, March 8, 2012.

12. "Who Am I? Issues relating to Identity Formation and Adoptee Adolescents," *Youth Studies Australia* 14, no. 1 (1995): 52, accessed January 11, 2013, http://ecite.utas.edu.au/6211/ and www.acys.info/_data/assets/pdf_file/0006/63996/p52_-_P._Westwood_-_March_1995.pdf.

13. Lynn Von Korff and Harold D. Grotevant, "Contact in Adoption and Adoptive Identity Formation: The Mediating Role of Family Conversation," *Journal of Family Psychology* 25, no. 3 (2011): 393–401, accessed March 2, 2012, https://docs.google.com/open?id=18GpHHrnlH60tbU89bhMbznf Edp88PFUx1-43qOMxTlJqJVzuoTdjM5w7_cIT.

14. *Wikipedia*, "Baby Scoop Era," accessed March 5, 2012, http://en.wikipedia.org/wiki/Baby_Scoop_Era.

15. "New Jersey Adoption Bill FAQs," accessed March 5, 2012, www.nj-care.org/legislation-faqs.php.

16. Jeanne A. Howard, Susan Livingston Smith, and Georgia Deoudes, "For the Records II: An Examination of the History and Impact of Adult Adoptee Access to Original Birth Certificates," *Adoption Institute Policy Brief*, July

2010, accessed March 8, 2012, www.adoptioninstitute.org/research/2010_07_for_records.php.

17. Adoptee Rights Coalition, "OBCs by State," accessed March 8, 2012, www.adopteerightscoalition.com/2001/02/colorado-birth-certificates-for.html.

18. South Carolina Department of Motor Vehicles, accessed March 5, 2012, www.scdmvonline.com/DMVNew/default.aspx?n=movingsc.

19. Child Welfare Information Gateway, U.S. Department of Health and Human Services, "Access to Adoption Records: Summary of State Laws," 56, www.childwelfare.gov/systemwide/laws_policies/statutes/infoaccessapall.pdf.

20. Travel.State.gov, The Service of the Bureau of Consular Affairs, U.S. Department of State, "First Time Applicants," accessed March 5, 2011, http://travel.state.gov/passport/get/first/first_830.html.

21. Find out how to support ARC's efforts at www.adopteerightscoalition.com.

6. HEADING TOWARD WHOLENESS: INTEGRATING YOUR CHILD'S BIOLOGY AND BIOGRAPHY

1. Portions of this chapter originally appeared in slightly different format at *LavenderLuz.com.*

2. "The Tale of the Ugly Duckling," *Parenting Your Adopted Child: Tweens, Teens and Beyond*, August 2, 2010, http://judymmiller.com/2010/08/the-tale-of-the-ugly-duckling/.

3. Jamie Lee Curtis, *Tell Me Again about the Night I Was Born* (New York: Harper Collins, 1996). For lots of great reading choices to suit your family's own circumstances, check out www.adoptivefamilies.com/books/index.php?cat=3.

4. Luna Sea, interview with Lori Holden, September 25, 2009.

5. Angie T., interview with Lori Holden, March 22, 2012.

6. Heather Schade, "Open Adoption Roundtable #16," *Production Not Reproduction*, May 27, 2010, http://openadoptionbloggers.com/2010/05/27/open-adoption-roundtable-16/. Explore letters other first parents and adoptive parents have written to their kids at this URL.

7. REALITY CHECK: WHEN IT'S NOT EASY

1. Portions of this chapter originally appeared in modified form at *LavenderLuz.com.*

2. *Wikipedia*, "Erik Erikson," accessed April 16, 2012, http://en.wikipedia. org/wiki/Erik_Erikson.

3. "Erikson's Psychosocial Stages Summary Chart," About.com Psychology, accessed April 17, 2012, http://psychology.about.com/library/bl_ psychosocial_summary.htm.

4. Deborah N. Silverstein and Sharon Roszia, Center for Adoption Support and Education, Inc., "Seven Core Issues in Adoption," accessed April 16, 2012, www.adoptionsupport.org/res/indexcorea.php.

5. While in this chapter we carefully mine the unique struggles facing adoptive parents and their kids, we devote all of chapter 9 to the birth parents, exploring in depth the issues they commonly confront.

6. Meg Kenning, interview with Lori Holden, April 14, 2012.

7. *Wikipedia*, "Reinhold Niebuhr," accessed April 9, 2012, http://en. wikipedia.org/wiki/Reinhold_Niebuhr.

8. *Dictionary.com*, "Bastard," accessed April 12, 2012, http://dictionary. reference.com/browse/bastard?s=t.

9. James L. Gritter, "Symposium 2011 Opening Adoption: Realities, Possibilities, and Challenges," keynote speaker, Richmond, Va., September 23, 2011.

10. Sara Harrison, interview with Lori Holden, January 29, 2012.

11. Interview with Lori Holden, April 18, 2012.

12. From www.bjlifton.com/counseling.htm, accessed April 13, 2012.

13. Andy Drouin, interview with Lori Holden, April 14, 2012.

14. Andy Drouin, interview with Lori Holden, April 14, 2012.

8. OPENNESS IN FOSTER, INTERNATIONAL, AND DONOR SITUATIONS

1. Mary Memmott, "Working with Birthparents [*sic*]," *Adoption and Foster Care: My Personal Experiences*, April 10, 2012, http://mamamem.blogspot. com/2012/04/working-with-birthparents.html.

2. Memmot, "Working with Birthparents."

3. Memmot, "Working with Birthparents."

4. Melissa Denton, interview with Lori Holden April 26, 2012.

5. Rachel Hoyt, "Family Is Family," *Eyes Opened Wider*, May 10, 2011, http://eyesopenedwider.blogspot.com/2011/05/family-is-family.html.

6. Hoyt, "Family Is Family."

7. Rachel Hoyt, interview with Lori Holden, April 29, 2012.

8. Rachel Hoyt, interview with Lori Holden, April 29, 2012.

9. "Openness in International Adoption," accessed May 1, 2012, www. adoptionrcc.org/OpenINTLadoptions.pdf.

10. Jennifer G., interview with Lori Holden, April 30 2012.

11. Nancy, interview with Lori Holden, April 30, 2012.

12. Judy Miller, interview with Lori Holden, May 7, 212.

13. Jessica O'Dwyer, interview with Lori Holden, May 8 2012.

14. Lisa Schuman, interview with Lori Holden, April 30, 2012.

15. Kami Kane, interview with Lori Holden, April 25, 2012.

16. Kami Kane, interview with Lori Holden, April 25, 2012.

17. Kami Kane, interview with Lori Holden, April 25, 2012.

18. Eric Schwartzman, interview with Lori Holden, April 30, 2012.

19. Eric Schwartzman, interview with Lori Holden, April 30, 2012.

9. ESPECIALLY FOR BIRTH PARENTS (AND THOSE WHO WANT TO CONNECT WITH THEM)

1. Callie R., interview with Lori Holden, January 26, 2012.

10. FARE WELL

1. Portions of this chapter originally appeared in a slightly modified version at *LavenderLuz.com.*

2. Great-Quotes.com, "Maya Angelou Quotes," accessed December 18, 2011, www.great-quotes.com/quotes/author/Maya/Angelou.

APPENDIX A: INSIGHT ON ADOPTION PROFILES

1. "Seven Tips to Review and Revise Your Adoption Profile" is reprinted with permission from ProfilesThatGetPicked.com, while "The Terrible Toos: Seven Common Mistakes in Adoption Profiles" is reprinted with permission from *LavenderLuz.com.*

BIBLIOGRAPHY

Adoptee Rights Coalition. "Colorado Birth Certificates for Adoptees: Who May Access Original Birth Certificate Information in Colorado." Accessed May 30, 2012. www.adopteerightscoalition.com/2001/02/colorado-birth-certificates-for.html.
Adoption Agency Ratings. "Adoption Agency Ratings." Accessed May 25, 2012. www.adoptionagencyratings.com/.
Adoption.com. "What Is an Adoption Agency?" Accessed May 25, 2012. www.adoptionagency.com/agencies/what-is-an-adoption-agency.html.
Anonymous. "How Does One Find an Ethical Adoption Agency as a Prospective Adoptive Family?" Open Adoption Support. March 21, 2011. Accessed May 25, 2012. www.openadoptionsupport.com/2011/03/how-does-one-find-an-ethical-adoption-agency-as-a-prospective-adoptive-family.
Axness, Marcy. *Parenting for Peace: Raising the Next Generation of Peacemakers.* Boulder, Colo.: Sentient Publications, 2012.
Beauvais-Godwin, Laura, and Raymond Godwin. *The Complete Adoption Book: Everything You Need to Know to Adopt a Child.* Cincinnati, Ohio: Adams Media, 2005.
Birth Mom Buds. Accessed May 25, 2012. http://BirthmomBuds.com.
Bullock, Sandra, Quinton Aaron, Tim McGraw, Kathy Bates, Lily Collins, and Jae Head. *The Blind Side.* DVD. Directed by John Lee Hancock. Burbank, Calif.: Warner Home Video, 2009.
C., Jessica. "Why Can't I Just Say No When Our [Birth Mother] Does Stuff That Is Not OK!" Adoptive Families Circle. February 1, 2012. Accessed May 30, 2012. www.adoptivefamiliescircle.com/groups/topic/3071/.
Cherry, Kendra. "Erikson's Psychosocial Stages Summary Chart." Accessed May 31, 2012. http://psychology.about.com/library/bl_psychosocial_summary.htm.
Child Welfare Information Gateway. "Access to Adoption Records: Summary of State Laws." Accessed May 25. 2012. www.childwelfare.gov/systemwide/laws_policies/statutes/info accessapall.pdf.
———. "Regulation of Private Domestic Adoption Expenses." Accessed May 25, 2012. www.childwelfare.gov/systemwide/laws_policies/statutes/expenses.cfm.
D'Arcy, Claudia Corrigan. "Is Your Adoption Agency Ethical?" *Musings of the Lame: My Life as a Birthmother and What I Learned Too Late.* January 27, 2012. Accessed May 25, 2012. www.musingsofthelame.com/2012/01/is-your-adoption-agency-ethical.html.
Davenport, Dawn. "Top Ten Warning Signs for Adoption Fraud." Creating a Family. Accessed July 9, 2012. www.creatingafamily.org/adoption-resources/adoption-fraud-warning-signs.html.

Davenport, Dawn, Kate Livingston, and China Darrington. "Difficult Dialogues: The Essential Conversations that Prospective Adoptive Parents Must Have Before, During, and After Placement." Also titled as "Birth Mother Panel: What First Moms Want Adoptive Parents to Know." Creating a Family. Recorded April 18, 2012. http://bit.ly/M7RUuy.

Dictionary.com. "Bastard." Accessed May 31, 2012. http://dictionary.reference.com/browse/bastard?s=t.

Drouin, Andy. "Family Trees." *Today's the Day They Give Babies Away!* October 19, 2009. Accessed May 30, 2012. http://todaysthedaytheygivebabiesaway.blogspot.com/2009/10/family-trees.html.

Great-Quotes.com. s.v. "Maya Angelou Quotes." Accessed May 31, 2012. www.great-quotes.com/quotes/author/Maya/Angelou.

Gritter, James L. *Hospitious Adoption.* Washington, D.C.: Child Welfare League of America, Inc., 2009.

——. *Lifegivers: Framing the Birthparent Experience in Open Adoption.* Washington, D.C.: Child Welfare League of America, Inc., 2000.

——. *The Spirit of Open Adoption.* Washington, D.C.: Child Welfare League of America, Inc., 1997.

——. "Symposium 2011 Opening Adoption: Realities, Possibilities, and Challenges." Keynote speech. Open Adoption Symposium. Richmond, Va.: Coordinators2, Inc., September 23, 2011.

Hagelstein, Brandy, May 5, 2008 (10:41 a.m.). Comment on GinaMarie119, "Adoption Application: Question Regarding Birth Mother Expenses." Adoption.com. May 6, 2008. Accessed May 29, 2012. http://forums.adoption.com/domestic-adoptions/333597-adoption-application-question-regarding-birth-mother-expenses.html.

Holden, Lori. "Adoption School, Day 2: I Am a Baby." *Drama 2B Mama.* October 19, 2009. http://drama2bmama.blogspot.com/2009/10/adoption-school-day-2-i-am-baby.html.

——. "Do Over: 'I'm a Bastard, Right, Mom?'" *LavenderLuz.com.* March 24, 2011. http://lavenderluz.com/2011/03/the-bastard-conversation.

——. "How I Embraced Open Adoption." *LavenderLuz.com.* May 4, 2010. http://lavenderluz.com/2010/05/how-i-embraced-open-adoption.

——. "Moments in Open-Adoption Parenting." *LavenderLuz.com.* November 3, 2009. http://lavenderluz.com/2009/11/moments-in-open-adoption-parenting-part-73-2.

——. "My Son Processes a New Layer of His Adoptedness." *LavenderLuz.com.* October 10, 2011. http://lavenderluz.com/2011/10/son-processes-his-adoption.

——. "My Son Speaks Adoption Language at School." *LavenderLuz.com.* October 5, 2010. http://lavenderluz.com/2010/10/son-adoption-language.

——. "On DNA." *LavenderLuz.com.* December 1, 2012. http://lavenderluz.com/2010/12/on-dna-nature-or-nurture.

——. "An Open Response to Anti–Open Adoption Sentiments: Part 2." *LavenderLuz.com.* April 12, 2011. Accessed May 29, 2012. http://lavenderluz.com/2011/04/why-i-am-pro-open-adoption.

——. "Returning to the Well." *LavenderLuz.com.* March 19, 2008. http://lavenderluz.com/2008/03/returning-to-the-well-2.

——. "Reunion in Open Adoption 3: A Different Kind of Wait." *LavenderLuz.com.* February 11, 2009. http://lavenderluz.com/2009/02/reunion-in-an-open-adoption-3-a-different-kind-of-wait-2.

——. "Reunion in Open Adoption 6: What Was the What." *LavenderLuz.com.* March 11, 2009. http://lavenderluz.com/2009/03/reunion-in-open-adoption-6-what-was-the-what-2.

——. "Two Women, One Daughter." *LavenderLuz.com.* September 12, 2008. http://lavenderluz.com/2008/09/two-women-one-daughter-2.

——. "What Does *Real* Mean: Adoption Talk with My Daughter." *LavenderLuz.com.* December 23, 2012. http://lavenderluz.com/2010/12/what-does-real-mean-in-adoption.

——. "What If?" *LavenderLuz.com.* April 23, 2010. http://lavenderluz.com/2010/04/what-if.

Howard, Jeanne A., Susan Livingston Smith, and Georgia Deoudes. *For the Records II: An Examination of the History and Impact of Adult Adoptee Access to Original Birth Certifi-*

cates. New York: Donaldson Adoption Institute, July 2010. Accessed May 30, 2012. www. adoptioninstitute.org/research/2010_07_for_records.php.

Hoyt, Rachel. "Family Is Family." *SocialWRKR24/7: Eyes Opened Wider*. May 10, 2011. Accessed May 31, 2012. http://eyesopenedwider.blogspot.com/2011/05/family-is-family. html.

Huffington Post. "John Wyatt, Father Fights for Custody of Daughter Who Was Given Up for Adoption without Consent." August 29, 2011. Accessed May 29, 2012. www. huffingtonpost.com/2011/08/19/john-wyatt-father-fights-_n_931311.html.

Independent Adoption Center. "Research about the Impact of Openness on Adoptees." Accessed May 25, 2012. www.adoptionhelp.org/open-adoption/research.

Kaufman Burns, Kate. "Openness and International Adoption: Creating Connections Across the Seas." Adoption Resources and Counseling Center, Inc. Accessed May 31, 2012. www. adoptionrcc.org/OpenINTLadoptions.pdf.

Lawlor, Jenn. "Looking in the Mirror." *Insert Bad Movie Title Here*. February 13, 2012. Accesed May 30, 2012. http://insertbadmovietitlehere.wordpress.com/2012/02/13/looking-in-the-mirror/.

Lifton, Betty Jean. "Counseling." *Betty Jean Lifton, Ph.D.: Author, Adoption Counselor, Lecturer*. Accessed May 31, 2012. www.bjlifton.com/counseling.htm.

LisaAnne. "How We Got Here." *Living Through Today*. September 23, 2011. Accessed May 30, 2012. http://lisaanne119.blogspot.com/2011/09/how-we-got-here.html.

Lowe, Heather. "Pre-birth Ties between Birth and Adoptive Families." Adoption.com. April 14, 2006. Accessed May 29, 2012. http://unplanned-pregnancy.adoptionblogs.com/weblogs/pre-birth-ties-between-birth-and-adoptiv.

McDermott, Mark T. "Independent Adoption." *The Adoption Guide*. Accessed May 29, 2012. www.theadoptionguide.com/options/articles/independent-adoption.

Memmott, Mary. "Working with Birth Parents." *Adoption and Foster Care: My Personal Experiences*. April 20, 2012. Accessed May 31, 2012. http://mamamem.blogspot.com/2012/04/working-with-birthparents.html.

Miller, Judy M. "The Tale of the Ugly Duckling." *Parenting Your Adopted Child: Tweens, Teens and Beyond*. August 2, 2010. Accessed May 31, 2012. http://judymmiller.com/2010/08/the-tale-of-the-ugly-duckling/.

———. *What to Expect from Your Adopted Tween*. Zionsville, Ind.: NliveN, LLC, 2011. Accessed May 25, 2012. http://judymmiller.com/the-book/.

NJCARE: New Jersey Coalition for Adoption Reform and Education. "New Jersey Adoption Bill FAQs." Accessed May 30, 2012. www.nj-care.org/legislation-faqs.php.

Pennell, Danielle. "'My Mom Tells Them How I'm Doing.'" Adoptive Families Circle. February 1, 2012. Accessed May 30, 2012. www.adoptivefamiliescircle.com/blogs/post/talking-about-adoption-birth-parent-letters/.

Pertman, Adam. "Study Shows Rise in 'Open' Infant Adoptions." Donaldson Adoption Institute. Accessed April 8, 2012. http://adoptioninstitute.org/media/20120321_openness_release.php.

Schade, Heather. "Open Adoption Roundtable #16: Imagining the Future." Open Adoption Bloggers. May 27, 2010. Accessed May 31, 2012. http://openadoptionbloggers.com/2010/05/27/open-adoption-roundtable-16/.

Schoettle, Marilyn. "W.I.S.E. Up! It's Back to School." Adoption Issues. Accessed May 30, 2012. www.adoptionissues.org/wiseup.html.

Silverstein, Deborah N., and Sharon Roszia. "Seven Core Issues in Adoption." The Center for Adoption Support and Education. Accessed May 31, 2012. www.adoptionsupport.org/res/indexcorea.php.

South Carolina Department of Motor Vehicles. "Moving? Welcome to South Carolina." Accessed May 30, 2012. www.scdmvonline.com/DMVNew/default.aspx?n=movingsc.

United States District Court for the Eastern District of Virginia. "Wyatt Complaint." Accessed May 29, 2012. www.babyemmawyatt.com/wyatt.Complaint1-19-11.pdf.

U.S. Department of Health and Human Services. "Access to Adoption Records: Summary." Accessed May 30, 2012. www.childwelfare.gov/systemwide/laws_policies/statutes/infoaccessapall.pdf.

————. "Adoption USA: A Chartbook Based on the 2007 National Survey of Adoptive Parents." Accessed May 25, 2012. http://aspe.hhs.gov/hsp/09/NSAP/chartbook/index.PDF.

————. "Postadoption Contact Agreements between Birth and Adoptive Families." Accessed May 30, 2012. www.childwelfare.gov/systemwide/laws_policies/statutes/cooperative.pdf.

————. "Regulation of Private Domestic Adoption Expenses." Accessed May 29, 2012. www.childwelfare.gov/systemwide/laws_policies/statutes/expenses.pdf.

U.S. Department of State. "First Time Applicants." Accessed May 30, 2012. http://travel.state.gov/passport/get/first/first_830.html.

Verrier, Nancy. *The Primal Wound: Understanding the Adopted Child.* Lafayette, Calif.: Nancy Verrier, 1993.

Von Korff, Lynn, and Harold D. Grotevant. "Contact in Adoption and Adoptive Identity Formation: The Mediating Role of Family Conversation Formation and Adoptee Adolescents." *Journal of Family Psychology* 25, no. 3 (2011): 393–401. Accessed May 30, 2012. http://ecite.utas.edu.au/6211/ and www.acys.utas.edu.au/ysa/index/au_w.html.

Westwood, Peter. "Who Am I? Issues Relating to Identity Formation and Adoptee Adolescents." *Youth Studies Australia* 14, no. 1 (1995): 52. Accessed January 11, 2013. http://ecite.utas.edu.au/6211/ and www.acys.info/_data/assets/pdf_file/0006/63996/p52_-_P._Westwood_-_March_1995.pdf.

Wetzstein, Cheryl. "Study: Families Trending toward Open Adoption." *Washington Times*, March 21, 2012. Accessed March 23, 2012. www.washingtontimes.com/news/2012/mar/21/study-families-trending-toward-open-adoptions/.

Wikipedia. s.v. "Baby Scoop Era." Accessed March 5, 2012. http://en.wikipedia.org/wiki/Baby_Scoop_Era.

————. s.v. "Erik Erikson." Accessed April 16, 2012. http://en.wikipedia.org/wiki/Erik_Erikson.

————. s.v. "Maslow's Hierarchy of Needs." Accessed February 22, 2012. http://en.wikipedia.org/wiki/Open_adoption.

————. s.v. "Open Adoption." Accessed March 21, 2012. http://en.wikipedia.org/wiki/Open_adoption.

————. s.v. "Reinhold Niebuhr." Accessed February 9, 2012. http://en.wikipedia.org/wiki/Reinhold_Niebuhr.

Zimmerman, Monika. "A Birthmother's Perspective." *See Theo Run.* December 28, 2011. Accessed May 29, 2012. http://seetheorun.com/2011/12/28/a-birthmothers-perpective/.

INDEX

adoptee: confusion, 140–141; identity,
100–101, 110–111, 132–133; intimacy,
141–142; issues (hitches), 138–145;
and peers, 91–93; and school, 93–94;
stories, 98, 99, 99–100, 140–141, 142,
144, 145. *See also* closed adoption;
roads not taken; trust
adoption language, 13–15, 73. *See also*
"bastard"; "real"
adoption professionals, 28–31, 31;
adoption agency, 30, 31; adoption
attorney, 31; adoption facilitator, 30,
31; questions for, 33–36, 37
adoption profile, 50–51, 183–187
adoptive parent, 13, 52–54; and absent or
reluctant birth parent, 176–178; and
birth parent pain, 136; and boundaries,
136; issues (hitches), 134–138; letter to
ask for more openness, 177–178; self-
assessment, 58–59
adoptive parenting: and absent or
reluctant birth parents, 137–138; and
birth parent contact, 113–115,
116–119, 122–125, 162; and
conversation about birth parent,
145–151; talking adoption with your
child, 119–122; and your child's
identity formation, 110–111, 112–113.
See also roads not taken
agreements, 85–86; broken, 75–78

amended birth certificates. *See* original
birth certificates
Anderson, Hans Christian, 109–111
answering questions about adoption,
83–84
Axness, Marcy, 64–65

Baby-Scoop Era, 6, 98, 103, 140–98
"bastard," 138–140
birth certificates. *See* original birth
certificates
birth family, extended, 125–126
birth father rights, 44–46
birth parent: adoptive parents' thoughts
about, 174–176; contact with placed
child, 113–115, 116–119, 122–125;
definition, 13–14; grief and grief
processing by, 61–63; issues (hitches),
169–172; letter to ask for more
openness, 172–174; responsibilities,
168; reluctance, 176–177; reunion with
placed child, 116–119, 122–125. *See
also* placing parent
The Blind Side (film), 156, 158
both/and thinking, 25–26, 115–116, 128,
179–180, 181
boundaries, 72–75, 84, 136, 181

closed adoption, 6, 82–83; and the
adoptee, 97–101, 140–141, 142, 144,
145

communication, 68–72
counseling, 151, 169–170, 172
culture. *See* heritage

DNA. *See* genetics
donor egg, 163–164, 166
donor embryo. *See* donor gametes
donor gametes, 163–166
donor sperm, 164–166

either/or thinking. *See* both/and thinking
Erikson, Erik, 132–133
ethics, 32–33, 40, 42–43. *See also* pre-birth expenses

failed match, 79–80, 135–136
family sculpting exercise, 55–56
fear, 1, 53, 54–52, 60, 61–62, 69, 81, 133, 170–172, 176
first parent. *See* birth parent
foster adoption, 153–159, 162–163, 166

genetics, 24–26, 101
ghosts. *See* Lifton, Betty Jean
grief, 53–54, 61–63, 65, 169–170
Gritter, James L., 1, 49, 65, 68, 71, 73, 140

heritage, 110–111
Hotel Rwanda. See Rusesabagina, Paul

identity. *See* adoptee
infertility, 52–54
international adoption, 111, 159–163, 166
intimacy, 141–142, 150. *See also* trust

Lifton, Betty Jean, 143–144

match meeting, 57–58
meditation exercises, 189–190
Miller, Judy M., 16, 110–111, 161
mindfulness, 65, 80, 90–91, 96–97, 138, 141, 147–151, 181, 189–190

nature vs. nurture, 25–26, 101. *See also* genetics
Niebuhr, Reinhold, 137–138

O'Dwyer, Jessica, 161–162
open adoption: benefits, 159; communication exercise, 60–61; definitions, 12–13, 16, 49, 56, 57, 68, 81, 102, 159–160, 161; embracing, 90–91; history, 4–6; ingredients for success in, 80–82; letter from the future exercise, 129; pros and cons, 18–19; self-assessment, 58–59. *See also* birth family, extended
open door adoption, 176–178
openness, 58–59, 113, 144, 145–151; without contact, 102
open records. *See* original birth certificates
original birth certificates, 102–106
otherness, 111–112, 166

Pertman, Adam, 3
placing parent, 54, 56–57, 59
post-adoption contact agreement (PACA). *See* agreements
pre-birth expenses, 39–44
pre-birth matching, 64–66; expectant parents deciding to parent, 135–136

raising siblings, 94–97
"real," 100, 127–129
reunion, 116–119, 122–125
roads not taken, 142–144
Roszia, Sharon, 133
Rusesabagina, Paul, 180–181

Serenity Prayer, 137–138, 172
Silverstein, Deborah N., 133

transracial adoption. *See* international adoption
trust, 144

"The Ugly Duckling". *See* Anderson, Hans Christian

Verrier, Nancy, 98

ABOUT THE AUTHOR

Lori Holden lives in Denver, Colorado, with her husband, her daughter Tessa, and her son Reed. She is passionate about yoga, about living mindfully, about coffee, dark chocolate, and red wine, and about de-freakifying open adoption. She welcomes contact from others exploring any of the above.

Blog: LavenderLuz.com
Twitter: Twitter.com/LavLuz
Facebook: Facebook.com/LavenderLuzWriter
Email: Lori@LavenderLuz.com
Google Plus: gplus.to/lavenderluz